C000022955

GREAT SCOTS
IN FAMILY BUSINESS

By Maurice Smith

BUSINESS BOOKS SERIES

Published in 1996 by Lang Syne Publishers Ltd, Glasgow, for Scottish Enterprise.

Printed by Dave Barr Print, Glasgow.

ISBN No. 1 85217 027 1

Contents

FOREWORD — v

INTRODUCTION — vii

BAXTER'S — 1
The Global "Village Company"

WALKER'S SHORTBREAD — 17
An independence engraved in stone

URQUHART — 25
A Century-old Whisky Dream Comes True

GERARD EADIE — 31
The Do It Yourself Millionaire

WISEMAN BROTHERS — 44
Pint-sized Ambition

TUNNOCK'S OF UDDINGSTON — 53
No Change to the Recipe for Success

BARR'S — 60
The Irn Bru Dynasty

RUSSELL TRANSPORT — 68
Two generations on the road

MALCOLM CAMPBELL — 76
A Family Business Adapting to the Future

ABEL EASTERN — 82
Phoenix from the Flames

MATTHEW ALGIE — 93
From Tea to the Gentry to Jive about Java

THE HALL FAMILY — 104
A Transition Success

FRED "MAGIC" JOHNSTON — 111
Falkirk's Unlikely Press Baron

FOREWORD

The majority of firms in most countries around the world are owned and controlled not by multiple shareholders, but by families. Scotland is no exception. Our country has been a breeding ground for international empires like the Wood Group, Walkers Shortbread, Stagecoach Holdings, whisky giants Grant's and the Irn Bru dynasty, to name but a few.

Few people realise that Scotland is home to an estimated 90,000 family-run businesses, providing jobs for more than 50 per cent of the country's workforce. That makes family businesses the backbone of the Scottish economy – the kinds of enterprises that make us great.

Dynamic Scots-born family businesses have shaped the lifestyles of millions of people around the globe, providing jobs, creating employment and bolstering the economy both at home and abroad.

Our proud industrial heritage has been built on the solid foundations of family-owned businesses. We now recognise these companies, their founders and successors as important role models for the next generation of budding entrepreneurs.

By inspiring a brave new breed of family enterprises whose energy and initiative may lead them to their own family fortunes, I am confident the success stories of some of our best-known family businesses will take Scotland closer to realising the goals of the Business Birth Rate Strategy.

That's what makes them worthy of the title 'Great Scots' and gives them their rightful place in the *Great Scots In Business* series of books, commissioned by Scottish Enterprise.

This book, the third in the series, traces family fortunes through the generations and showcases the success family enterprises have earned through hard work, careful planning and determination.

From Teviot founder Brian Hall, whose first tiny office was so dingy that fungus seeped through the floor, to Walker's of Aberlour – a company which started as a village bakery in 1898 and now boasts a 600-strong workforce and a staggering annual sales figure of £40 million – all the stories in this book trace the highs and lows in the lifetime of a business, from the dream of winning the first major contract to the despair of watching profits plummet.

Some of them started in a back room or, in the case of W.A. Baxter and Sons, in a modest village shop. Nevertheless, all have turned an idea into a working enterprise which will not only provide security for the controlling family, but also employment and wealth for its workforce.

Exploring complex family relationships in a business setting, *Great Scots in Family Business* also profiles the businessmen and women in control of today's best-known family enterprises and gives a fascinating insight into how they overcame a series of hurdles on the fast track to success.

The book points out that, according to accountancy firm BDO Stoy Hayward, just 24 per cent of family businesses survive the hand-over to second generation and only 14 per cent make it to the third. I pay tribute to the various members of families like the Campbells, who have taken their fruiterer business, Malcolm Campbell, into its fifth generation.

The company which introduced the banana and tomato to Scotland at the turn of the century has been tailored to meet the ever-changing demands of a highly competitive market. Under the control of the founder's great, great grandsons, Malcolm Campbell Ltd is now an £8 million business with a 200-strong workforce.

Only by learning from the experiences of companies like Malcolm Campbell will future family enterprises outlive their founders and grow with each new generation.

However, this book is much more than a reference guide for established business families. It is an historic helter-skelter of highs and lows, a study in survival and a tribute to the founders and successors whose family empires have placed Scottish business on the worldwide map.

Great Scots in Family Business is an exhilarating and inspiring account of the steadfast resolve of Scotland's champions through the generations. Its stories will grip the dreamers and transform them into achievers.

Russel Griggs
Business Development Director
Scottish Enterprise

INTRODUCTION

We do a lot of lamenting in Scottish industry. We lament the loss of heavy manufacturing industry, and its great icons such as the Clyde-built liners or the locomotives which helped millions traverse the great old Empire. Today we struggle, with good reason, to comprehend the implications of our greater dependence for employment on the service industries, or on the foreign manufacturers who populate Silicon Glen.

Being Scottish, we are able to lament the loss of headquarters' control of great companies who have succumbed to external takeover, often in hostile circumstances. Yet we can also complain that so few Scottish companies opt for a Market listing at all. And still we can cheer if, for example, Scottish Power completes two hostile takeovers of English companies, or one or other of our banks manoeuvres successfully to retain its independence against hefty odds.

There are good reasons for all these contradictions. One telling explanation is that in lamenting so many losses, or complaining about this or that trend whenever it is seen to act against the Scottish interest, we are in fact sharing a worldwide bewilderment at the speed of change across every industry. Change is unsettling, and experiencing a great deal at once, as every industrialised nation has done during the last 20 years, can be demoralising. We all experience vulnerability. In Scotland we express that fear by lamenting the apparent frailties of our economy. Sometimes we blame the English, just as the English blame Europe, the Americans blame China, and Russians blame the West in general.

These are legitimate concerns. But what we fail to do often in Scotland is celebrate our successes. Apart from our few manufacturing survivors, and our strong financial services sector, we have probably neglected the one sector which continues to create jobs and exploit external markets with greater success than any other: family businesses.

The Scottish economy was built on owner-managed enterprise. Many of the great names who collapsed or sold out or were acquired "in takeover battles" throughout this century were family companies originally. Yet Scotland has many survivors, who thrive, often as household names. They provide thousands of jobs between them, and these are often far more secure, far more entrenched jobs than those which are "parachuted in" from abroad.

This book profiles 13 such companies. It also examines what motivates Scotland's entrepreneurs, and what quality it is that keeps them independent. Many have made their names by establishing a firm hold on "niche markets", such as specialist foods or regionally-based services from milk distribution to double-glazing. Two of them - Johnston Press and A.G. Barr - are even public companies now, but still managed by their founders' descendants.

They vary from start-up companies such as Gerard Eadie's C.R. Smith to others which stretch back several generations such as W.A. Baxter & Sons. This book attempts to explore how families work together, and most importantly how they approach the crucial point of survival for all owner-managed businesses: the succession of management from one generation to another. They all have interesting, sometimes exciting, stories to tell, and those stories should be inspiring to anyone in business, or thinking about setting up on their own. I have attempted to include a spread of businesses with varying experiences. There are many more examples in Scotland, and - who knows - there may be another opportunity to tell their stories in another book some day.

Family companies sometimes can be reluctant to speak in public. Many of them prefer to operate privately; often that is their very motivation for remaining independent. But I have experienced nothing but courtesy and generous assistance from those who participated here, and would like to place on record my thanks to all those who agreed to be interviewed. For people whose lives are absorbed in running a business, it can feel awkward to sit for hours talking to a relative stranger about their experiences, and sometimes their personal feelings. But everyone here did so with aplomb.

In addition I would like to thank Chris Baur and Alastair Balfour of Scottish Business Insider for their part in setting me off on the family business trail, initially for the magazine; Russel Griggs and Gordon Beattie for their backing and encouragement; Barbara Dunn and Kate Lanka at the Centre for Family Enterprise at Glasgow Caledonian University; and my own family, Wendy, Catherine, and Julie.

Maurice Smith
Glasgow, August 1996.

Maurice Smith covers business affairs for BBC Scotland, and is a regular contributor to Scottish Business Insider. He spent 10 years in Scottish newspapers, latterly with the Glasgow Herald, before joining the BBC in 1989.

CHAPTER ONE

The Global "Village Company"

The images of Gordon and Audrey Baxter fill the giant screen in the 100-seat auditorium at their company's visitor centre, filmed as they tell a prestigious business conference in London's Royal Albert Hall about the compelling virtues of being small and beautiful.

Gordon, typically proud, has just told the Institute of Directors about the Highland success story whose reputation is worldwide. W. A. Baxter & Sons, a small village store which started a sideline in jam making, then soup and pickled beetroot, is now a £50m business with more growth to come. He describes the experience of running the company, all mock modesty, as "a love affair".

The company chairman, now its president, tells the pinstripe-suited audience of merchant bankers and politicians: "My daughter Audrey and I have travelled from the little Speyside village of Fochabers, 200 miles north of Edinburgh and 650 miles north of here." It is a familiar tale of homespun enterprise. Baxter almost always makes a virtue of being small and remote: the reality of the company's growing presence on the supermarket shelves of Europe, America and Australasia tells another story today.

The Baxters arrived in tiny Fochabers, eight miles east of Elgin, Morayshire, in 1740. Gordon's grandfather George opened a village store in the late 19th century, and started to make jam for the local market in the back-store. Gordon's parents, William and Ethel, opened a factory in 1916, and took advantage of improved transport communications to market the jam further afield.

William, a consummate salesman, had won orders for Ethel's preserves from Harrods, Fortnum & Mason, the Army & Navy Stores, and even Buckingham Palace. A buyer from the New York store with Scottish origins, Macy's, spotted the goods in Harrods and placed the Speyside firm's first export order. Then in 1929 Ethel provided the breakthrough by developing Baxter's first true brand - and one which remains a supermarket favourite today - Royal Game Soup.

And so the video of the conference presentation continues. Pleased as Punch, Gordon Baxter long ago became an expert at selling a product range which is inextricably entwined with the company's history. He sells on the concept of Scottish quality, on the perception of Scots as canny, thrifty, honest, and committed to providing the best food on the market. At 78, his selling instincts are as strong as they were on the day he stepped off a plane in post-war North America and realised where his little Highland company's future lay.

The Albert Hall video is one of several on show to the tens of thousands of tourist visitors who come to Fochabers each year to witness Scotland's most famous family business in action. The company president points out that where once there were 2,000 independent grocery firms to supply, the market has boiled down to a few giant supermarket chains and the discount houses. The 20 Scottish jam-makers of 1945 are now just two; of 40 soup-makers in Britain then there are now just three - "two of them foreign-owned", says Baxter, and there is no need to ask which is the third.

The company now exports to 30 countries, and has survived by product innovation and a fierce sense of independence. Baxter reveals his company has received no fewer than 172 takeover inquiries during his 47 years at the helm. When the video was recorded, he was in the throes of handing over the day to day management of the business to his daughter Audrey, a successful former merchant banker who returned to Fochabers in 1987 after a great deal of agonising, and is now determined to make Baxter's a £100m company by the Millennium.

Then the finale. As if to emphasise the point of the whole presentation - the Baxter company's independence, its continuing reliance on family business values, the commitment to longevity and quality service - Audrey returns onstage with her six week-old daughter, Catherine Mhairi, to tumultuous applause and a standing ovation. "The next speaker asked me 'how am I going to beat that?'" recalls a beaming Gordon Baxter.

We are sitting in his father William's former bedroom in the original Baxter home, which serves now as company headquarters. Several years ago Gordon bought a set of display cases from a retired antiques shop owner in Perth, and began to create what he describes as a "shrine", in that old bedroom. The glass fronted cases are stuffed with company artefacts and memorabilia: Letters from noted customers, cans with their original labels from the 1950s, advertising early successes like Chicken Gumbo Soup, Baxter's Haggis, or Whole Roast Pheasant. The labels vary according to the language and the periods during which they were produced. The shrine includes an archive of every letter, document, product line and event which has had an impact on Gordon Baxter's life. He and his former secretary, now in semi-retirement, meet weekly to file and store each little chapter in the company history.

The choice of room is appropriate. In 1947, Gordon's father William decided to retire at the age of 70. His elder son had not long returned from wartime duties in the armaments industry and with his brother Ian had been struggling to find raw materials and new markets. "He took the keys from his desk, handed them to me and said 'now Gordon, you do it', as simple as that," recalls Baxter, who was then 28. But the older man, even years later when he became a widower, continued to take an intensely detailed daily interest in the company. Each evening in his bedroom he pored over copies of every piece of correspondence and every invoice that had passed through the offices below. Beside his bed he had a pile of pre-printed notepaper with the red-letter legend "Don't Forget". Each morning his son would receive a neatly-written pile of notes gleaned from the nightly forest of paperwork.

William Baxter continued the habit until his death, aged 96, in 1973. When the company commissioned a massive and still comparatively rare IBM machine in 1954 - a clumsy electro-mechanical precursor of today's ubiquitous desktop PC - it had to be reconfigured to provide those vital copy invoices for the old man upstairs. William continued to turn out at company events, such as the opening of a rebuilt version of his father's original village store in 1968. The photograph adorns the company library. "My father and I got on very well. He was a great friend as well as my father," explains Gordon. "He had a great retentive memory, and I had an interest in history. Everything he told me helped me to restore his shop and reopen it at the visitor centre as a reminder to the family about the humble beginnings we came from." So was created a second family shrine at Fochabers.

In a corner of the archive room is a bookcase bearing several expensive hand-bound leather volumes which record the family history, intertwined as it is with that of the company. There are photographs of the children, of Gordon and his wife Ena in glittering company at New York's Waldorf Astoria, or aboard the Cunard liner Queen Elizabeth; and Gordon and brother Ian at Buckingham Palace where the chairman received an OBE.

Among the volumes are a few devoted to the plethora of takeover inquiries which have arrived at Fochabers since the 1950s. Their tone varies from the obsequious to the direct. Many are from merchant banks, brokerages, and other middlemen, usually declaring their interest on behalf of an anonymous client. Their style was normally a mixture of condescending flattery and an attempt to impress Baxter's with the potential bidders' great wealth. Gordon has attached appropriate, often whimsical remarks beside every one of them.

Those suitors who are still identifiable today make up an impressive "Who Was Who" of Britain's industrial great and good back through the last four decades: Sir Hector Laing of United Biscuits; a young James Gulliver, prior to his creation of the successful Argyll foods group which was to include Safeway; the late Sir Hugh Fraser, before he blew the millions inherited from his father, Lord Fraser of Allander; and Charles Villiers, later head of British Steel but then in charge of Industrial Mergers Limited, an off-shoot of the investment company that became 3i.

The company names look familiar too: Batchelors, Rowntree, British Vinegars, Shipphams, Standard Brands, Distillers, General Mills, and the American owned Libby, McNeill & Libby. Strikingly, most of these once-great commercial names were to succumb to takeover themselves. The late Sir John Toothill, acknowledged as the father of the modern Scottish electronics industry, is recorded as passing on a notice of interest on behalf of a business acquaintance. There is another inquisitive note from a member of the Baring family, of Baring's Bank fame.

Perhaps the cheekiest approach was from a Dutch based broker, who wrote several letters advertising a book which it described as "The Acquisition Manual for Baxter's of Speyside Limited", retailing at $9,950. The broker offered the book rather brazenly to Baxter's at a special discount "for one copy only" of $5,990. If this was an attempt either to impress or intimidate that "little village company" which Gordon so cleverly portrays, Baxter's recorded reply is suitably brief and to the point.

Gordon Baxter has amassed so many such approaches that he jokes that his autobiography should be entitled: "200 - Not out". The truth is that, since his resistance is so widely and publicly recorded, the number of inquiries may never reach that magic total. Only the thickest-skinned predator could have missed the point that this company, of all companies, has no intention of selling out.

The US foods giant Heinz is among those who would like to own Baxter's. Its Irish-born president and chief executive, Dr Tony O'Reilly, a multi-millionaire newspaper publisher and businessman in his own right, has visited Fochabers and discussed the matter, at least half-seriously. His host took him fly-casting on the Spey. Whatever O'Reilly caught there, it was not to be the Baxter empire.

Gordon Baxter was made company president in 1994, as the company entered a new phase in its history. A new production plant was commissioned at Fochabers, and the family management team was put in place after lengthy spells of apprenticeship. Eldest son Andrew is vice-chairman, and the youngest, Michael, became a director in recognition of his skills in public relations and product development. The Baxters' middle child, Audrey, was confirmed as managing director, amid great publicity, something she attributes as much to her gender as to anything else.

The switch to president represented an acknowledgement on her father's part that finally it was time for Audrey to take over. But full retirement is not really an option for Gordon Baxter, 42 years older than his daughter. The age-gap is unusually large, just as it was between Gordon and his father, and the recent appointment of a former managing director of the food chain Sainsbury, Joe Barnes, was probably an attempt to bridge the gap before Audrey is left in complete charge. At 36, she has time on her side.

"There are three children and five grandchildren, so I think the company is safe for another 50 years," remarks Gordon. And then he adds, candidly: "I will work on as long as they will have me. I think I would die if I had nothing to do. I am an adviser and friend, and the nice thing is that the children still like to talk to Ena and me about the business."

The children are three quite different personalities. The eldest, Andrew, now 38, takes charge of production matters and information technology. A quiet man with a dry sense of humour, he took a BSc in business management and has spent almost his entire career with the firm. He is acknowledged within the Fochabers management team as "a rock, very solid". His father says Andrew is a "solid character". His brother Michael says of him: "Andrew has always been into computers and motorbikes. He used to be forever taking engines apart and putting them together again."

Michael, aged 33, is fascinated by the process of food itself, in its ingredients and recipes. One of his ambitions is to write a book about the nature and history of raw ingredients. A former semi-finalist in the BBC TV programme Masterchef, he is acclaimed by the others as an innovative cook and the source of many new ideas as the Baxter range continues to broaden annually, as part of the company's continuing drive to stay ahead of market trends against intense competition.

Amongst all the company landmarks and personal mementos, the Fochabers archive includes family snapshots of the three children, taken in the 1960s. They appear to conform to their adult personalities: Andrew, aged around 10, tall and looking slightly awkward; Michael, shy with blond curls and, as the youngest, clinging to the others. Audrey stands out as the centre of attention, her jaw set, determined looking even in childhood.

The pictures were taken as their parents were in the midst of turning Baxter's into an international force. The company owes its success to a couple whose meeting after the last war sparked a partnership which pushed Baxter from the corporate backwater of the Scottish Highlands into today's modern global supermarket. For years they travelled the world in search of new customers and ideas, and by the time they decided to retire it had all paid off.

The company's origins were quite typical. George Baxter, a gardener on the estate of the Duke of Richmond and Gordon, borrowed £10 and opened a grocery store in Fochabers in 1868. His wife Margaret made jam in the back-shop, and their son William realised its popularity meant it might be sold farther afield. He started supplying stores as far north as Wick and east to Aberdeen. Distrustful of the mails, for years he relied on train drivers and guards to collect his orders from clients in Aviemore and Fort William, and drop them off at Fochabers junction, on the Aberdeen to Inverness line.

William married Ethel Adam, a local woman remembered by Ena Baxter as "physically strong and completely dedicated", who turned out to be the catalyst for the company. The Baxter factory opened in 1916, with the help of the Duke, who owned the land, two years after William and Ethel's marriage. For the next 25 years Ethel dominated the business, expanding production and working long days alongside her tiny staff, leaving her husband, described by his son Gordon as "a real silver tongued salesman", to find new markets. "My mother was a heroine, and a slave to the business," believes Gordon. Family legend has it that Ethel single-handedly made three tons of blackcurrant jam just two days before giving birth to her first son in 1918.

Ethel developed Royal Game Soup and another modern mainstay, sliced beetroot, whose popularity is such that even today Baxter's supplies 40 per cent of the UK market. Its genesis was the result of a chance meeting, as is so often the case with milestones in every company history.

William made a routine visit to a long-standing client, the manager of a Banff wholesaler called Graham & Company, which tended to supply groceries and wines to the local gentry in the affluent north-east. The manager took Baxter to a store, whose ceiling was pock-marked with glass shrapnel and deep purple staining. A Glasgow supplier had failed to sterilise its jars properly, with the result that they had fermented and exploded, leaving beetroot and glass splattered everywhere around the store. "Can you do something about this?" the manager asked William. The enterprising Baxter said yes, and then checked with his wife back in Fochabers as to whether something could in fact be done.

Pupils at a Grampian reform school were digging crops as part of their duties. William Baxter ordered half a ton to be delivered to Fochabers railway station. Ethel cooked the lot, sliced it by hand, and stored it in vinegar. A new, long-lasting product-line had been launched, as simple as that. As a schoolboy Gordon lost the tip of a finger while operating a slicing machine, and had it sewn back on in hospital in Elgin. By then Baxter's was shifting a lot more than half a ton of beetroot, and today it can be bought in every possible form: sliced, crinkle-cut, whole baby beets, and so on.

Gordon and his younger brother Ian grew up in that environment. As their mother worked, they were cared for by a succession of nannies hired in nearby Buckie. But the business was everything, and for as long as they can remember the boys played, then worked, around the Fochabers factory.

The elder son was advised by his father to take up accountancy or science, two skills that would be useful to the business. He opted to study biochemistry at Aberdeen. When war intervened, he was called up and an unexpected use was required of his chemistry skills: rather than going to war, he was sent to Imperial Chemical Industries' explosives plant at Ardeer in Ayrshire to help develop new armaments, taking over production there before war ended.

Baxter returned home in 1946, soon to receive the keys to the business from his father. Things were far from healthy, as wartime austerity and post-war rationing threatened to undermine the company itself. Baxter's employed 11 people - a far cry from the 800 of today - and annual sales were just £40,000. The company had just £4,000 in the bank. The potential for growth was hampered by the restrictions imposed by the new Labour Government as Britain struggled to revive its economic fortunes. Victory exhausted Britain: six years of rationing and the need to direct industry to the war effort left the country in a weakened state, barely capable of restoring its prewar strengths.

"The Ministry of Food ran everyone's life," recalls Gordon Baxter. "We had no machinery, no money, and the supply of raw ingredients was limited to prewar usage. We found it difficult to obtain sugar, tins, jars, paper for labels, everything in fact. During the war people like Crosse & Blackwell and Heinz had taken on war contracts and had plenty of everything. I remember having to crawl to the Metal Box Company to buy 5,000 cans, whereas today we buy tens of millions. I had to crawl to United Glass for jars. It was a hell of a job."

Improvisation was king. Baxter contacted municipal sanitary inspectors around Scotland and offered to pay them for glass jars collected locally. Soon inspectors in Glasgow, Falkirk, Girvan, Uddingston, and elsewhere were sending second-hand jars north to Fochabers. Each had to be checked, broken ones discarded, the rest washed and rewashed before Baxter's could use them for jam. The firm returned to profit, marginally, in 1947.

Despite the pain of the time, Labour's austerity provisions were to offer an unexpected glimpse of the future for Gordon a few years after war's end. "Socialists are not all that bad sometimes," remarks Gordon today. "The Minister of Food, John Strachey, produced a scheme under which for every ton of sugar we used to make jam for dollar markets we got an extra ton for use in the home market. I knew then I should try my luck in Canada."

The company's survival was to depend on exports. Baxter contacted two friends in the food sector, George Crawford, who ran the Gray & Dunn biscuit factory in Glasgow's Kinning Park, and George Hitchen, of Duncan's Chocolates in Edinburgh. They passed on the names of their agents in Canada, and Gordon was on his way to creating a commercial legend. He stepped up production of jam and preserves back in Fochabers, appointed an agent in Vancouver, and set off to explore new markets.

"I made a thousand mistakes," he recalls, adding characteristically: "Well not a thousand but certainly a few." Baxter's jam was shipped to Vancouver via the Panama Canal, and the equatorial climate there caused the syrup to expand. "The Canadian agent, Arthur Richardson, spent his Saturday mornings mopping around the tops of the jars and removing syrup from the labels with a cloth. We had got the caps wrong. He really saved the day I think."

Gordon meanwhile had met Ena Robertson, a farmer's daughter from Huntly in Aberdeenshire, whose interest in art had taken her to Fochabers as a teacher. Having studied art formally, Ena had been forced to change tack during the war, and worked in the Food Ministry's laboratory at Torry in Aberdeen. Little did she know that the knowledge gained there would influence the rest of her life.

"I met and married Gordon, and I knew of the Baxter company, but did not realise at the time that he *was* the business," recalls Ena. "I found him fascinating because he was the type of man I had always been looking for. He had an integrity and a tremendous ambition to be successful. I think he inherited that."

Aged 26, Ena married Gordon in King's College Chapel in Old Aberdeen in 1952. It was the beginning of an intense partnership where marriage and children were entwined with the fortunes of the business. Ena accompanied Gordon on business trips, she entertained buyers and clients at the family home, and took a high profile role in the company's progress, even presenting her own cookery slots on a Grampian Television programme, much later on.

Just as with her mother-in-law's experience with beetroot, Ena became involved directly in the business after experimenting in her own kitchen, the result of a chance encounter involving her husband. Gordon had visited the food hall of a prestigious London client, Selfridge's, to check on his products' progress on the shelves. He came across a newly-published New York food magazine called Gourmet, and the edition carried a feature entitled, "The Song of the Soup Kettle". Thinking his wife might like to subscribe to it, he brought the magazine home to Fochabers. Sometime later he returned from work one evening to be presented with a tasty soup which Ena had drawn from a recipe in the magazine. It had the peculiar name Chicken Gumbo.

"If you can make more of that, I think I could sell it," declared Gordon. Ena set about experimenting further, but with difficulty. The Gumbo recipe demanded okra, a vegetable to be found in India, Africa, and the West Indies, but not in Speyside. The couple had to look the name up in their dictionary.

Eventually Gordon secured some tinned okra, and the recipe was augmented with green beans from the Fochabers garden. In addition there was the problem of attempting successfully to "scale up" the ingredients from a home recipe to the requirements of mass production.

"When we first tried to can it we really did not have the technology or the experience to do it properly. There was a lot of trial and error before we could get it right. But in year one we sold one million cans," remembers Ena. "The British public was tired of the wartime diet. Anything new on the shelves was eagerly taken up."

So the company turned the corner by its successful development and marketing of a soup whose recipe was based on one provided in a foreign magazine and whose own origins are in the American Deep South. Necessity was truly the mother of invention. Ena quickly found she was no longer married to the business, but becoming an essential element of its progress.

The couple revamped Ethel's Royal Game Soup, with fewer spices, more wine and meat content, and followed the advice of the grocery buyers, who said that to succeed the company would have to introduce contemporary favourites such as Scotch Broth and Cream of Tomato. The Highland preserves company had become a national soup manufacturer in an intensely competitive market almost overnight, and soup still accounts for 50 per cent of all sales today. "So much of the other companies' product was dull and predictable: Cream of Chicken, Cream of Mushroom, and so. We knew we had to offer something different," points out Gordon.

The next breakthrough was to come during the late 1950s and early 1960s. Ena remembers travelling to the United States in 1958 in a De Havilland Comet: "The plane that was always crashing. I was never so relieved to see dry land." Her husband had become more and more fascinated by the American experience.

Unlike Britain, America had prospered quickly after the war. Its economy was booming, and the food sector was at the vanguard of growth. Ahead of the rest of the world, American food manufacturers and distributors were learning to move quickly as a result of the massive economic and social change brought about by technology and prosperity. Markets were expanding, whole cities were developing quickly. The automobile had transformed communications, and America was witnessing the beginning of the "urban sprawl" phenomenon, where citizens moved from the centre of town and out to new housing areas. These "new" consumers were to be found in the shopping malls and early supermarket chains.

It was to be a long time before Baxter's exploited the US market in a meaningfully successful manner. The company was too small to take on the likes of H. J. Heinz in the race to fill the market shelves. For the next 25 years Baxter's greatest source of sales growth would remain in Britain. But Gordon

Baxter learned a lot about marketing in North America which was to stand him in good stead back home. "The United States really opened our eyes to the wider world," affirms Ena.

In Chicago, Baxter met the head buyer for the Jewel Tea company, based in the city's Melrose Park. The buyer was a Dundonian called Scottie Wilson, and he had earned vast experience in the US, wielding enormous power when it came to negotiating with would-be suppliers such as Baxter. "It was a cold bleak winter's day in 1959. Wilson presided over a great army of buyers, he sat in a glass box looking like Santa Claus with my samples of jam. He listened to me and admired the samples," recalls Baxter.

"But then he said 'Gordon you come here all the way from Fochabers with your mother's jam and your wife's soup. I need these products like a hole in the head. Have you ever heard of the word marketing? Have you discovered what it is that the American consumer actually wants? Go and find out, and then I will buy your products'.

"That was it. I went back to Fochabers and turned this business upside down."

The penny had dropped for Baxter. His little family business had worked hard and turned out new products. It had earned respect. But it remained very small. "Instead of just carrying on the thing was to find out what the trends were. Although I was an introverted chemist I had to become a salesman, and marketing became my passion. So many Scots do not advertise their product - they expect the consumer to come along and buy it. And another thing I learned was that you have to set out to be the best," reflects Gordon.

His experience in Chicago was one that he would never forget, and the resulting philosophy is instilled in Baxter's today, as is obvious from its vast modern product range and its instinctive determination to keep launching new products onto an increasingly dynamic market. Ask Audrey or Michael about the company's plans today and their answers will seem entirely consistent with the salutary lesson delivered to their father by that tough-minded Scots-American back in 1959, before either child was born.

A key player in the change of direction was Ena. The part-time cook who dabbled with recipes became an important agent within Baxter's itself. As Gordon trod the marketing path, travelling worldwide in pursuit of orders, his wife was attempting new products as a matter of routine. The celebrated food writer Margaret Costa once wrote a profile headed: "What's for Dinner Mum?' where she portrayed the Baxter children as guinea-pigs at the Fochabers kitchen table. "There were always experiments going on," remembers Audrey. The utility room in the Baxter home contained hand-operated canning and bottling machines; Audrey remembers it as "a fantastic playground". Her mother says: "All the soups we produce are as near home-made as it is possible to get. I did test them out on the children, and they would always give straight answers."

Gordon became the marketing whizz, but Ena was in the front line of the advertising campaigns. She wrote "Ena Baxter's Scottish Cook Book", which continues to be popular, and apart from her early experiences on local TV, has also appeared live in her cooking apron on American cable TV. In the UK, Ena and other family members and staff have featured in TV advertising. The image is familiar and comforting, playing heavily on Baxter's relatively remote home base and its environmental attractions. The voice-over says: "When this woman makes soups, she only uses the finest raw ingredients." Reassuring. Traditional. In fact, exactly the image Gordon Baxter has chosen to portray his family business.

The marketing strategy has always been helped by its veracity, by the fact that the "Baxter story" is rooted in real life rather than hyperbole. Fochabers is a small working town in the midst of some of Scotland's most attractive scenery and close to one of the world's great salmon rivers. Gordon, a keen angler, jokes that the main qualifications for his non-executive directors are that "they must be able to fish the Spey!" The visitor centre, completed only recently, attracts more than 200,000 visitors yearly not just because of the Baxter name, but because it is on a popular tourist trail. If Scotland wanted to invent a locale specifically with quality in mind, Speyside would probably provide the answer. In advertising and marketing terms, Baxter's achievement has been to use its headquarters location to the greatest possible advantage.

"I think it is always reassuring to the market that there is a family behind the brand. After all, there is no Mrs Oxo or Mister Maxwell House," remarks Michael Baxter.

Michael, at 33 the youngest of the family, comes across almost like the ambitious middle manager chafing to rise through the ranks of a giant food corporation. His enthusiasm for the brand, for its potential, is infectious. He delights in talking about the details of the product development kitchen at Fochabers, and enjoys visiting London to entertain the food editors who dine out on Baxter's as a familiar passion. The company's reputation for quality within the industry is very real.

Like Andrew, Michael appears to have found a niche in a company still dominated by their father in many respects, but which is inevitably going to become identified more closely with Audrey, a woman who evidently shares Gordon's leadership instincts. "Audrey was the one to be managing director," says her mother. "That was always quite clear."

The Baxters pride themselves in keeping up with market trends. They introduced vegetarian soups just as the market was beginning to demand non-meat alternatives; sugar-free jams were another first. Gordon initiated the "mini-pots" of jam and marmalade so common in hotels and within in-flight meals today. Audrey herself is credited with having initiated the idea of the

"Healthy Choice" range: high-fibre soups with strong appeal in overseas as well as home markets.

"We are stepping up the innovation," believes Michael, who worked on his uncle Ian's farm, then in property development in Edinburgh and in the kitchens of the Hong Kong Hilton Hotel, before returning to Fochabers. "We would not have been doing products like Cream of Red Pepper or Spicy Thai Chicken with Lemon Grass (two recent new soups) before, but we have to keep up with trends in the market place."

Michael's job is to "read" the market, in other words to detect trends and changing tastes and adapt the Baxter's range to suit. Apart from using his instincts, he keeps close tabs on the industry and talks to the food writers - a very influential group in both Britain and the US - regularly. In a sense, his job is a more formal version of the experience of his grandfather William when he spotted a niche for beetroot, or countless similar examples involving Gordon and Ena since the 1950s.

In one year, the company plans to introduce no fewer than nine new soups, all of them accepted in advance by the supermarkets. He thinks there will be further growth in desserts and condiments. "We can get a soup out very quickly. I think people like Heinz are too bureaucratic: if I have to, then I can get a product in and out of our kitchen and into the market within three months," he adds.

For Gordon Baxter, there is still much in which to remain engaged. The recent completion of the visitor centre at Fochabers - initiated when he restored his grandfather's village store on the new site several years beforehand - has been a source of fascination and pride. It attracts an average of 205,000 visitors each year, having opened in 1986.

Tourists can marvel at the company's history, or its Queen's Award for Export Achievement, or its three Royal Warrants. They can follow guided tours of the factory itself. Apart from the "old shop", there are three more, selling Baxter foods, kitchenware and utensils, or Scottish crafts. The centre includes a 180-seat restaurant and the auditorium includes audio-visual presentations in several languages. Half a mile west of Fochabers itself and housed within the Baxter's complex, it is almost a "village within a village".

Gordon personally has been identified with the company for so long that standing down would have been a painful decision, however appropriate it may have been. He clearly enjoys his new title as company president. A friend, wine trader Sandy Irvine Robertson introduced him affectionately at a Scottish Business Achievements Awards event several years ago, describing Gordon as that "greatly loved, benevolent autocrat - Lord Baxter of Beet!"

The process of handing over the reins has been slow, and perhaps rightly so, although the perceived wisdom within the family business sector is that management succession should be planned well in advance, and not when the chairman is in his seventies. Audrey returned in 1987, and was clearly the anointed successor. But Gordon stayed on as chairman until 1994, when Audrey was confirmed as managing director, and Joe Barnes was recruited as chairman. A respected figure in the British industry, Barnes is clearly there to sponsor Audrey's attempts to spark further growth, as well as bridging the age gap between father and daughter.

Unusually for a family firm, Baxter's has several non-executive directors, and recruited them before corporate governance became an issue in Britain. "I pride myself that I always knew when I needed advice," says Gordon, who became president when Audrey moved up. Ena stepped down too, having continued to work in the factory lab, where she and Gordon once experimented on new recipes with just the ingredients, some cutlery, and a Bunsen burner. She wanted to spend more time with her first love, art, having established a reputation as a notable still-life painter.

The company's adoption of non-executive directors was another idea learned during the early 1970s from an American example. Gordon aimed to recruit big names, and that probably helped build respect for the company too. His current non-executives include Sir Jan Lewando, formerly of Marks & Spencer; Ronnie Lagden, former European president of Quaker Oats; and David King, former chairman of SmithKline Beecham Brands in the UK. Chairman Barnes also served previously on the Baxter's main board.

Audrey, 36 and married with a child, is determined to push the company towards an annual turnover of £100m soon after the turn of the century. She points out that since she rejoined the business sales have risen from £26m to £48m, and she still discerns enormous potential in the British market alone.

She had left Fochabers as a teenager, to school in St Andrews, and then studied economics at Heriot-Watt University in Edinburgh not because of a special interest, but simply because she had failed to get a good enough biology grade to study science at Aberdeen. "I wanted to do genetic research, and suddenly I was doing economics, but I loved it," she remembers. "However when I came out the last thing I wanted to do was join Baxter's - I was 23 and I wanted to make money."

She moved to London, with three offers of employment in the burgeoning financial services sector as a graduate trainee. This was 1983, in advance of "Big Bang", when the Conservatives de-regulated the financial markets and helped usher in one of the biggest financial booms in history, albeit a short-lived one. Audrey was an analyst with the City firm Kleinwort Benson, commanding a big salary and being tipped for promotion. She was among a growing number of women to break through in the City during that period, and several old girlfriends have since moved nearer the top within the banks and institutions there. "I think when I told Dad I was going to London he was disappointed momentarily, but supported me. Mum used to introduce me as 'my merchant banker daughter'. I think they were quite tickled by it," she says.

The decision to return was momentous, even though Audrey concedes that she had always expected to return sometime. "I agonised. I am very independent. I did not want to come back to a closed community - remember I had not lived in Fochabers since I was a little girl," says Audrey. "I was in my mid-20s, single, had been living in London in my own place. I knew I would be under a microscope in our company. But if my heart had not called me back my head would have said 'what are you doing?'

"I suppose I felt by then that I had something to bring back to the business. That was important to me personally. The bank had wanted me to move overseas, and when I visited Fochabers there seemed to be something going on, new products coming out, and things like that. I felt quite isolated from the family."

Audrey's return attracted a great deal of publicity and interest from the Scottish business community. Suddenly she was being invited to speak at conferences and seminars or join business lobby groups and other committees. She believes that much of the interest was simply because of her youth and her gender. She says pointedly: "I learned a lot from all that", but adds that the higher-profile had a positive side, allowing her to get involved in directorships and projects outside the family firm.

Her first task on arriving in Fochabers was to draw up a five year strategy for the company, an important acknowledgement in itself by Gordon that the business needed to be revitalised. "You have to set short and medium term goals. The goals for this company are to grow the business profitably and within our own finances. I do not see Baxter's as a massively acquisitive business, growing through ferocious financial transactions. But the core of the business has a lot of growth left in it," says the MD, her merchant bank training showing through.

Audrey has introduced new standards for personnel management and marketing within the company. Her father says that she proved quickly to the company that she could handle a crisis, such as when the parent company of Baxter's Australian distributor faced collapse and Audrey flew there to sort out an alternative.

She believes she has identified two specific markets which Baxter's should exploit more forcefully, partly because of the firm's growing relevance as a "niche" player specialising in high quality foods which appeal to increasingly health-conscious consumers. The first such market is Australia, and the second involves carefully-selected regions of the United States, such as Boston, Massachusetts, Philadelphia, the Washington/Baltimore area, and the North western states. Above all, these are food buying areas whose shoppers are influenced by trends and fads. With its short lead-times, Baxter's believes it is more capable than most in adapting to such fast-changing tastes. The company is especially popular among middle and upmarket shoppers belonging to the ABC1 social and economic classification.

Audrey is more likely to seek alliances to help foster that new marketing drive, especially abroad. "It is a part of modern business culture anyway, and the cost of bringing a new brand to the marketplace can be astronomical." What will not be traded is the company's equity. The family retains 98.6 per cent of the company, the balance held by non-executives. Gordon and Ian transferred their holdings to Gordon's children, and the bulk is held in trust. Baxter's is virtually impregnable.

"We always remember that Britain is still an exciting food market. In world terms it is still the best retailing market and we are very well placed within it."

But what of the transition? As Audrey had feared, her return to Fochabers did indeed put her "under the microscope", as she raced to learn every aspect of the business. "Dad was very much the patriarch and ruled almost autocratically, which was fine because it worked. But it took me two years to find my feet," she says, adding that she did admire Gordon when he took the final decision to step down.

"Dad did have a very open mind. He was always very fair to us all as children, treating us equally. We are good friends, probably because we think alike. He is a comrade in business because my worries and issues with Baxter's are very often ones that he had to deal with before. He will listen and counsel.

"From a business sense it is important that he takes a backward step because sooner or later there would have been a clash. Our styles are so different that if we were close in running the company together that would not have worked."

She was fortunate in that her arrival coincided with the reformation of the company's marketing department, something Audrey took on. It allowed her to work more closely with big clients such as Sainsbury and Tesco, both of whom take Baxter's product as well as contracting the Fochabers firm to provide their "own label" specialities.

She has come to rely on her brothers at a time when the company's expansion is taking hold. Their bid to rejuvenate the product range, expand production with a new factory, and virtually double sales is a bold one. Audrey makes it clear that she is in charge, but acknowledges the support her brothers provide.

"We have important roles. They both understand that the decisions are made through my office, but Andrew very much has his own mandate on the plant and capital side, and Michael has his mandate with the PR and creative side, which he is superb at. We just make sure we are aware of what each other is doing.

"We are three very different people but our reasons for being in the company are the same. We have good friendships and we can talk. I would hate to be in a situation working with brothers or sisters who have fallen out so much that they do not even talk. I know that can be rife in some businesses."

Audrey observes that growing up within a family business can be difficult: very often a child will feel obliged to prove that they are employable by working elsewhere at least for a while. "I think if you are a member of a family business you have to be true to yourself. If you are not happy in the company, or frustrated or whatever, do not be afraid of taking money out of the business, if the profit is there, and changing your life. There can be a fear of leaving a family company, because it is a very enclosed comforting environment. I have seen in other companies people who commit themselves when secretly they would rather be doing something else."

Audrey has collected non-executive directorships with two City investment trusts, the Scottish Exhibition and Conference Centre in Glasgow, and the National Stadium project. "I think it is quite important for the next generation of a family company, once they are established and comfortable with what they are doing, to get exposure in other companies.

"One of the risks I see with family businesses, and it could have happened in Baxter's, is that you can become quite isolated in the family environment. We run Baxter's like a public company, quite deliberately. You have to have a few disciplines in place. We are already panning for the next generation."

The new generation of Baxters have five children between them, all too young to be considering careers in the business. But Audrey insists that they are already being planned for, as an additional spur to succeed. "I do see myself as a caretaker of Baxter's for the next generation. I want them to have what our parents have given us: a beautiful business which is poised for the next stage of growth. If I can do that I will have done well."

Baxter's of Speyside is that quintessential Scottish family company. It understands the value of its history in the modern market place, and uses it to great effect. But if you ever meet Gordon Baxter, do not let him kid you that this is a backwoods' firm that somehow got lucky: it got where it is today by a firm adherence to quality and an eye for the consumer. Baxter's is a truly global "village company".

CHAPTER TWO

An independence engraved in stone

D rive through the simple, solidly-built and respectable Speyside village of Aberlour and your only passing thought may be that it is like so many others in the north of Scotland. A couple of hotels, banks, post office, and a few havens for souvenir hunters. All in all a typical little place on the road between the busier neighbouring towns of Elgin and Grantown upon Spey.

The only clue to Aberlour's wider influence may be found at an unusually well-appointed bakery store in the main street. Walker's of Aberlour, founded in 1898, is stuffed with the widest variety of shortbread, biscuits, cakes, meringue cases and souvenirs. All packaged in a striking and increasingly familiar red tartan. This is clearly no ordinary village bakery.

Follow the clues, and less than half a mile south you will come across one of Scotland's most important independently-owned food exporters. Three factories employing 600 people work round the clock to supply 40 per cent of the UK shortbread market and 60 per cent of its export market. A further plant devoted to manufacturing cookies has been added recently, just 20 minutes' drive away in Elgin.

Walkers Shortbread has won numerous awards across Europe, and was twice recipient of the Queen's Award for Export Achievement in 1984 and

17

1988. The company enjoys annual sales of £40m - twenty times the level of 1980, when Walkers was undergoing a massive change in direction - and continues to return impressive profits.

At the heart of this marketing phenomenon stand two brothers and a sister, Joe, James, and Marjorie Walker. They are both the board and senior management of this innovative food manufacturer, having taken over from their father James and uncle Joseph during the 1970s. Ownership is guarded jealously, so much so that voting shares can be held only by those actively involved in the company. Rarely, in these days where great attention is being paid to corporate governance in industry, Walker's Shortbread does not include a non-executive director. Everything is kept in-house, although James signals in conversation that the issue may be under debate, and could change to some extent in future. What will not change is the company's resolute determination to remain independent.

The three have always divided their activities with the intention of achieving best effect rather than duplication. Joe, who began work in the Aberlour bakery first, in 1958, specialises in managing production, an area of massive growth during the last two decades. Marjorie takes care of finance, administration, and personnel. James, who joined with Marjorie in 1962, heads marketing.

Now all in their fifties, the Walker trio have begun thinking about the future. Joe has three children in the business already. A fourth, son Nicky, is nearing the end of a long professional footballing career, having served as goalkeeper for Rangers, Motherwell, Hearts, Partick Thistle and latterly Aberdeen. He is expected to join the firm in a management role whenever his sporting career comes to an end, although it should be noted that goalkeepers tend to survive the pressures of the professional game rather longer than outfield players.

Marjorie's son David chose his own career in farming - he breeds Aberdeen Angus cattle - and James's four children are still too young to be planning business careers. But Joe's other two sons and daughter Philippa are involved actively: Philippa and newest recruit Richard in product development; Andrew managing the Elgin cookie plant. Although there are several other senior managers - most of whom have never worked anywhere but Walkers - the family retains a firm grip on the business.

The shortbread factories appear almost brutally efficient, although the Walkers point out that their operation remains labour intensive because of the fact that so much of their product is hand-finished, an essential factor in retaining quality. The quality mix of butter, sugar, and flour - the key to Walker's success - begins its passage at one end of a long line of machinery, and millions of shortbread and biscuit variations are packaged at the other end.

Walker's original "Pure Butter Shortbread" is produced in seven varieties: fingers, petticoat tails, rounds, triangles, and other variations of mix. Added to the product range are shortbreads peppered with chocolate chip, hazelnuts or almonds, enrobed in chocolate, flavoured with stem ginger or made with wholemeal flour. New products include shortbread biscuits flavoured with Australian macadamia nuts, and "Ginger Royals".

The key to Walker's success is its use of butter. The company's growth, fuelled in James's words by "aggressive marketing", can be traced back to the mid-1970s, when Britain and Europe suffered butter shortages, a far cry from the scandal of the "butter mountains" many years later. "Some of the biscuit manufacturers started using margarine instead of butter because it was cheap and more easily available. More and more people came to us after that period," recalls James.

The original Joseph Walker started his bakery in 1898, and it was typical of the period, supplying a limited market within roughly a 25 mile radius. Walker had a reputation for hard work and quality baking, and although his business strategy was unadventurous by modern standards, it was a worthy survivor when the founder retired and handed over the reins of the business to his sons, Joseph and James, in 1930. Their greatest task was to ensure the business survived the austere times of World War Two and post-war rationing.

The sons worked hard. They believed however that their father had stayed on in control for too long, and were determined not to make the same mistake when it came to the next management succession. Joseph had no children, and passed on his shareholding to his brother's children, Joe, James, and Marjorie. "My father and uncle created a base that was easy for us to develop," believes James. "Although we were all still quite young, they saw how hard we were prepared to work in the business, and eventually made the three of us partners. That motivated us to give our best."

As the children learned their trade during the 1960s, and prepared to take over during the next decade, they assumed that growth was to be had simply by expanding the bakery business, and opening more shops in the Speyside and Moray areas. Their shortbread was almost a sideline, and did not supply the UK market adequately, while exports were unheard of. Joe and Marjorie had young children then, but James was still unmarried, and more willing to travel further afield. But the three were convinced that growth could be had by increasing production and attacking the wider market in new ways.

They decided to stick their necks out, and attempt to market shortbread particularly in untested fields. James, the youngest and just turned 30, decided the direct approach was the best: after all, the provincial Scottish company then had little or nothing to lose. James approached the buyers from the food hall at the world famous London department store Harrods. And even though Harrods still operated its own in-house bakery then, it agreed to take on Walker's shortbread line: a big boost for the little Speyside operator. "I got great kicks out of that back then," recalls James.

Inspired by the Harrods' success, the family took the same approach to the department store sector in North America, and won orders from giants like Saks and Marshall Field. Little did the Walkers know that ultimately they would be serving more than 40 export markets.

Inevitably they decided to extend the bakery in Aberlour, and lodged a planning application. Instead, the then Banff County Council offered them a field to the south of the village. The company's explosive growth was about to be set in train. Production began in 1975, when the first export orders began to filter through.

"We had developed the business initially as a general bakery, with new shops in places like Elgin and Grantown. But it continued to be very seasonal and we continued to be dissatisfied with our progress," explains James. "We were convinced that our shortbread had the greatest potential, and that there could be a national market for it. People already knew us for our shortbread, in London and Glasgow for example."

The most important task was to differentiate Walker's product from that of its competition. The Walkers were beginning to understand the advantages of developing their company's brand image. They may have been inspired by the success of their near neighbour in Fochabers, W.A. Baxter & Sons, whose grasp of marketing was particularly sophisticated by the standards of the time.

It is not unusual today for a hotel guest anywhere in Britain to find that the "self-catering" shelf in their bedroom might include a packet of Walker's cookies, a plastic mini-pot of Baxter's jam or marmalade, and tea and coffee sachets stamped with the legend Matthew Algie & Son: all three are among Scotland's small but successful legion of family companies operating in the food sector. The brand name has become intertwined with success and helped build these companies' market presence across the UK.

By 1975 Walker's had become much better equipped to fund, achieve and sustain growth. The respected Speyside bakery business was about to become a national brand. It was a period which would test the Walkers' own personalities, and their abilities to communicate properly and work together well. Annual sales had reached £250,000 and the company was employing 100 people, many of them the wives or daughters of men working in Speyside's numerous whisky distilleries. It was a tight-knit community, and the company was certainly a biggish fish in a very small pool.

Joe's skills at supervising production would be tested when the extended bakery was replaced by a fully-fledged factory assembly line. Marjorie would be managing the finances for growth - a crucial test - and supervising recruitment as the workforce expanded. James, boosted by his early success with Harrods, which contracted Walker's to make the store's "private label" (also known as "own label") shortbread, had to build on that foundation quickly. Collectively, the Walkers had to justify their investment and the risk attached to it.

The company attended its first overseas trade fair in Germany, and the reaction of one suitably impressed local buyer was to teach James a salutary lesson. The German, who had clearly experienced problems in the past, dealing with British companies who had made great promises but failed to deliver, challenged Walker's to prove it would still be in the market in 10 years' time. "He liked our package, but he needed to know he could be sure of supply. That was a lesson I have never forgotten," recalls James.

"Breaking though into a new market can be slow, and if you chop and change things too often it can do you a lot of harm.

"For an export market a salesman is only as good as his factory back home. It must be able to deliver and cater for the market. Pretty brochures do not sell the product on their own."

By 1980 Walker's was already selling £2m of shortbread products annually, a growing share of it overseas. The introduction of a proper production line in the Aberlour factory had allowed the company to ensure greater consistency of quality. Various attempts had been made on the British and foreign markets by other, usually larger, manufacturers, but it became very obvious that their key failing had been quality. To buyers in the increasingly powerful British supermarket chains, or the American department stores, Walker's represented the answer: high-quality ingredients and a commitment to quality which crossed from the selection of raw materials to the delivery itself. "We were quick to take any advantage that came our way," emphasises James.

The company hands out an embroidered card, similar to a formal invitation, which sets out its simple but fundamental rule: "We guarantee this shortbread to be manufactured from the finest quality creamery butter, fresh eggs, and the choicest ingredients possible to obtain. No margarine or other substitute is included in the recipe." Simple but effective, in a harshly competitive world where far larger biscuit manufacturers, having witnessed Walker's "niche" success in the specialist market, have attempted to copy its products, largely without success.

Alongside shortbread, the Walkers found a similar national and international appetite for oatcakes, supplying many world-famous names, and even manufacturing a brand developed for the commercial arm of Prince Charles's Duchy of Cornwall.

Today, the three factories at Aberlour churn out more than 10,000 tons of shortbread each year. The total workforce varies according to season, at between 550 and 800 people, making Walker's one of the most significant employers in the north of Scotland. Eighty people work in the new Elgin plant, which was built in 1994 to include additional capacity with further expansion in mind. It is a long way from the early part of the century, when Joseph Walker supplied local customers by horse and cart, and a journey to Elgin was a veritable expedition.

During the 1980s, when new business came quickly, Walkers expanded the product range hugely, introducing chocolate and wholemeal products, as well as meringues and cakes: the latter having been bakery store products which had not joined the Aberlour production-line during the initial growth years. The range includes Dundee cake, Scotch Bun, Paradise cake and Strathspey fruit cakes. The pride of the range is the Glenfiddich cake, cooked with ingredients including the famous Speyside malt whisky of the same name.

They pay close attention to market trends, and pride themselves in the fact that new products can be brought to market quickly. In recognition of the distinctiveness of some American markets such as New York City, for example, they had their products approved and registered as Kosher. The sweetest range, including cakes rich in fruit and butter, is especially popular in the Middle East and Gulf states. Specific products have been prepared for Europe and Australia, two current growth areas.

The Walkers guard jealously the home-spun image of a family company operating in the remote Scottish Highlands. It is very seductive with customers at home and abroad. One company brochure claims proudly that new products - which roll off the lines with great regularity - are tested by local consumers, because they are offered for sale first at the now-restored bakery store in Aberlour village.

Although the production lines appear pristine and awesomely efficient, the Walkers baulk at the suggestion that this might be a factory like any other factory: devoted to efficiency above all else. And here they have a point: the quality of Walker's products is undisputed, and a large part of that success is the result of a production process which aims at perfection. Quality checks are frequent, and there is a cheerful atmosphere on the shop floor. The employment of so many people in production - administration accounts for less than five per cent of the workforce, an impressively lean overhead - means that quality can be maintained, and that new products or varying market demands can be acted upon extremely quickly.

A key point has been the development of the brand itself. Walker's products are so heavily branded, the packaging so ubiquitous, that even shortbread made as "private label", in other words packaged under the name of Saks or Harrods or Neimann-Marcus, is identifiable as having come from the Aberlour line.

The rich red tartan which adorns almost all of Walker's packaging has helped strengthen that image. The Walkers name is usually depicted in white, shadowed in gold, and carries the legend: Product of Scotland. Established 1898. Alongside at the top of each packet is a ribbon effect graphic, including a detail from a celebrated painting, "Flora MacDonald's Farewell to Bonnie Prince Charlie" (Isle of Skye, 1st July 1746), by S. Joy. The more upmarket tin

tin containing a shortbread selection reproduces the painting in full, and even in a matt finish surrounded by gloss: an expensive packaging option. Other 18th century oil paintings depicted on Walker's products include a portrait of Charles Edward Stuart (the Bonnie Prince) and another showing Mary Queen of Scots being serenaded by a lute-playing Lord Darnley.

The historical theme has been utilised across much of the range. The Walker's boardroom is furnished with display cases stuffed with every part of the range - dozens of products - contributing to a mass of red tartan images on cardboard. It is all part of a clearly defined and studiously implemented policy. To the Walkers, the name should instantly conjure up traditional images of quality and history in the mind of the consumer. Their centenary year in 1998 provides a further opportunity to underline the point.

But in addition to that, the range includes a few more modern innovations. A German promotional pack uses a scene from the movie Rob Roy, featuring Liam Neeson and Jessica Lange. "Der Keks Sum Film!" declares the text, claiming an effective if rather tenuous link for Walker's biscuits.

For the Japanese market children's biscuits are packaged in illustrations from the character Peter Rabbit: a popular story series in Asia. Much more adventurous is a recent tie-up with the Disney Corporation. Young consumers at Disney's retail stores and theme parks can now buy a shortbread product called "Mickey's Shorts-bread" - biscuits imprinted with the famous cartoon mouse's equally familiar shorts.

Alongside the colourful packaging, there are boxes of shortbread, chocolate biscuit and oatcakes featured with some of the world's leading brand names: Fortnum & Mason, Wedgwood, Harrods, Sainsbury, and Caviar House. In addition to the Duchy of Cornwall, Walker's biscuits are now packaged for sale by the National Trust. The company's whole branding and packaging effort is geared towards retaining the consumer's perception of Walker's as a "blue chip" quality name.

"What we have developed now is a strong packaging statement and a very strong brand which is the result of 20 to 30 years of effort in a consistent fashion. I am a great believer in the phrase 'if it ain't broke, don't fix it'," says James.

Back in Aberlour, the unpretentious trio at the heart of this success story remain unassuming. Joe is friendly but reticent, Marjorie formal, friendly and polite. They leave James, a youthful 52, to do the talking normally. And, although their personal rewards are suitably high, they believe their unpretentious lifestyles reflect their commitment to the business rather than on lining their own pockets.

The firm is resolutely independent. One potential suitor confided once that, having the examined the company's structure, he had given up the idea of a takeover. That suits the Walkers, who have no intention of selling out, having ensured that the shareholding structure is impregnable.

"I think our commitment to hard work motivates the staff. They see that we do not have glamourous lifestyles, and that every penny of profit is reinvested. We are creating jobs and providing for future growth," says James. "The most important thing is that the money is not going down to some corporate head office somewhere."

The two brothers and sister meet daily, sometimes formally for "30 minutes in the boardroom", more often on the factory floor or the office corridor. The key issues to be addressed daily are in ensuring supplies of raw materials and packaging, and in addressing any problems raised by customers. Although all three are joint managing directors, Joe chairs meetings where necessary, having the slight edge in experience. "It is a lean management. We have always had a fear of creating an unnecessarily large structure. We rely on senior managers for advice, and there are no non-working directors," adds James.

He refers to the staff as "incredibly committed", and confirms that the company attempts to build on the family-orientated foundation, because many families themselves work for the Walkers. As an example, James has recently appointed a secretary whose father is a driver for the firm, and whose mother works in quality control. Eleven of Walker's 16 senior managers have spent their working lives there.

The company recently bought out its long-standing North American distribution agent, based in Long Island, New York. The owner set up the business in 1960, and his association with the Scottish firm stretches back to 1975. The family reasoned that owning the distribution network in such an important market would "bring us closer to the customers".

James believes in keeping the driving philosophy simple. "We have to learn to keep up with change in the future. I think we offer continuity coupled with a constant desire to improve.

"You cannot help looking around and remembering companies who have sold out because they only had one product. On the other hand there are those who have diversified too far, and switched resources too frequently with the result that they neglected their core brand or product line. It is a balancing act."

The current shares' structure was devised in the early 1990s, with the resolute aim of incentivising future generations who remain actively involved, while keeping other family shareholders content with regular dividends.

"This is a way of life for each of us, rather than a job. It is our total commitment, being both work and a hobby," explains James Walker. "Everything is done with the intention of staying independent. It is a top priority, because we think that is good for our customers and employees. We do not even discuss any other possibility because it is engraved in stone that we keep the company independent."

CHAPTER THREE

A Century-old Whisky Dream Comes True

For 12 years the Benromach whisky distillery near the ancient town of Forres lay redundant, unstirred, its demise the result of a major shake out of Scottish production caused by the big players' need to reduce capacity and raise stocks during a period of falling demand.

The decision by the former Distillers Company to cease operations at Benromach, and several other old Scottish distilleries, was a cause for great lament in the industry, not just because of the reduction in jobs, but because the enormous ructions which had hit the whisky sector during the late 1970s and early 1980s threatened to undermine its very being.

As Western tastes switched from "brown" spirits like whisky to "white" ones such as Bacardi and vodka, and as wine sales soared, it seemed that the little distilleries which had been such an important part of of the social and economic fabric of Highland communities were doomed to fail. The whisky industry was shrinking fast, and becoming increasingly dominated by the big distillers, who were succumbing themselves to foreign ownership. The entire sector appeared to be vulnerable, and there was a great feeling of doom across the board.

Benromach closed in 1983, after more than 70 years of production. Ironically, during the intervening years, whisky has boomed, and the boom was led by the old Distillers company, renamed United Distillers after its bitter and controversial takeover by Guinness. Prices went up, and whisky was marketed as an upmarket brand, demanding a premium in Western markets, and - most importantly - enjoying soaring sales in new markets such as southern Europe, India, south-east Asia, and Latin America. Whisky had survived its worst downturn since American Prohibition, and was prospering even better than before the slump: sadly, Benromach had been an early casualty, and there seemed little chance of a revival.

Still the Speyside distillery remained silent, a source of anguish to George Urquhart, chairman of the Elgin-based wholesalers Gordon & MacPhail. Despite being 74 years old and in the throes of handing over the the company he had inherited from his father to the next generation, Urquhart bought Benromach in 1993, with high hopes of restoring the whisky to its rightful place on the grocery shelves by the turn of the century.

The distillery's aged oil-fired distilling equipment had been removed, but in a way that suited George and his four children, who have since taken over the company's management. They installed smaller stills and began production in 1995, with the first malts expected to be available in the year 2005 or 2007. The re-opening is the culmination of a personal dream for George Urquhart, but it also seals a historical link, closing a circle between times past and present for Gordon & MacPhail.

The Elgin company had long purchased Benromach whisky by the cask, and bottled it in their store in the city's South Street, before shipping it around Britain along with dozens of other local brands. The distillery purchase will make it possible for the company, created in 1895 by two enterprising local businessmen, James Gordon and John Alexander MacPhail, to re-establish a direct link with its own past. Hopefully it will bring a worthwhile single malt to market into the bargain.

"It has always been our wish to have a distillery," explains George's eldest son Ian, aged 49, who took over as managing director of Gordon & MacPhail when his father retired in 1993."It has always been seen that this would be a good thing for the company, and given our history it seemed logical to buy one."

Luckily for the Urquharts, who bottle and blend whiskies from nearly three dozen local distilleries, they still have a stock of Benromach, dating from before the closure in 1983. Until the new brand comes on stream in the early part of the new century, they are distributing the older supply as a vintage malt.

Ian and his brothers David, 44 year old UK sales director, and finance director Michael, aged 42, run a company with annual sales of £9m. Each spent a long management apprenticeship under their father's tutelage. George remains company chairman, but in virtual retirement, having started with Gordon & MacPhail as a junior member of staff in South Street. As a 14 year old, George watched from below as the whisky casks from a plethora of

Speyside distilleries were rolled down a ramp from the street into the basement, where the task of bottling would begin. Working there at such a tender age, he learned the trade quite literally from the "bottom up".

Most consumers purchased their whisky from local grocery stores such as that in South Street. "Whisky arrived in five gallon jars. People would bring in their own bottles and ask for a gill or a half gill measure," says George. The business also had contracts to supply food to hospitals, schools, and hotels.

The original shop remains, refurbished and still an important wines and spirits' store for the area, as well as a tourist attraction. Gordon & MacPhail operates now from much larger premises beside Elgin City football ground in Boroughbriggs Road. The family-owned company's board is completed by George's daughter Rosemary, aged 51, and non-executive director Harry Cathcart, a former corporate finance specialist who ran the Scottish arm of the Hill Samuel merchant bank.

Elgin was an important Highland town in the latter part of the 19th century. Today it continues to thrive. A new wealthy merchant class had developed in Speyside, thanks to improved transport links and communications with the outside world. Major companies such as Walker's Shortbread, W.A. Baxter & Sons, and the whisky distiller William Grant & Sons still have their roots there, as do many other well-known firms in food, textiles, and engineering. Back in the 1880s and 1890s, several whisky distilleries opened locally: they were to create an important new economic base.

The prospering new local gentry wanted the best of everything: cheeses and meats were imported from Britain and Europe, and fine wines too. The north of Scotland may have seemed remote to the salons of Paris and London, or even Glasgow, but railway links were improving and trade followed the money north.

It was boom time for the nascent whisky industry. Scotland's national drink boasted a few recognisable brands, but much of it had remained barely one up the ladder from poteen in terms of quality and consistency. Many of today's established names may claim grander origins, but the fact is that often a distillery would emerge from a family farm whose owner had originally set up a still in the corner of one of his fields.

By the latter half of the 19th century, whisky was on an upswing. Brandy had been the dominant spirit across Europe for generations, but crop failures and the disease phylloxera, which destroyed many vineyards, had combined to push up prices. Drinkers sought an alternative, and whisky provided the answer. There was an explosive growth of distillers around the Highlands and Islands of Scotland. Enterprising Scots were marketing their blends - rather than today's more fashionable and sought-after malts - far beyond their home territory. They were helped greatly by access to the burgeoning and accessible markets of the British Empire.

James Gordon was a typical product of the Speyside enterprise culture. A travelling salesman, he developed the idea for a licensed grocery, and teamed up with MacPhail. He had identified the fact that all the new distilleries would need a wholesale and retail outlet, and calculated the opportunity. The scheme was not without problems, the principal one being a Mrs Crowe, secretary of the local branch of the British Temperance Movement, who attempted to block the new company's licence application.

Eventually, the local magistrate approved the licence, and soon the local newspaper, the Elgin Courant & Courier, carried a formal notice of the new business, which stated: "The groceries, wines, and spirits are all High Class Goods, and Customers favouring them with their Patronage may depend on getting a superior article at a popular price". In modern times, that might be described, just as grandly, as the firm's "mission statement".

Gordon had a keen nose for good malt whisky, and built a thriving business whilst negotiating hard-nosed deals with the new distilling entrepreneurs. His acumen helped Gordon & MacPhail escape the worst effects of the so-called "Pattison crash" of 1899, when the fraudulent dealings of an Edinburgh blending company led to its collapse and a severe dent in the entire industry. The banks got nervous, and distillers paid dearly for their over-production, as prices collapsed. Several distilleries closed and many merchants faced ruin.

The Elgin business opted to remain within the trade, even though its whisky stocks had depreciated virtually overnight. Ian Urquhart believes: "The founders must have been very entrepreneurial, because we know they were marketing whisky as far away as London within two years of opening." The connection with today's management was established in 1915, when MacPhail retired and Gordon offered a former apprentice, John Urquhart, his partnership. Gordon died suddenly while driving his car in Elgin soon afterwards, and his widow took over half of the business until her retirement around 1920. Urquhart's grandchildren run the company today.

His son George must have enjoyed the realisation of a long-held dream when he supervised the purchase and re-opening of Benromach in the 1990s. For between the war years his father frequently debated whether or not to buy just such a distillery before deciding instead to concentrate on building relationships with by-now established names such as Glenlivet, Macallan, Glen Grant, Mortlach, Linkwood, Strathisla and Longmorn.

John Urquhart knew the whisky trade well, probably because his apprenticeship was served both with Gordon & MacPhail and with a separate whisky brokering business run by James Gordon. But the company also sustained its grocery business, remaining a wholesaler right up until the 1990s despite the sea-change in groceries caused by the growth and ultimate supremacy of the supermarkets in Britain.

The company stocked up on malt whisky during the inter-war years, defying market trends even when whisky sales were depressed: exports of whisky were damaged badly during the years of American Prohibition. The Depression added to the gloom, and many whisky communities faced economic collapse. John Urquhart, as much from a sense of duty rather than anything else, continued to buy whisky, in order to keep many small distillers in business. The gamble paid off during the Second World War, when Gordon & MacPhail released a large part of its stock in order to earn export dollars from the United States.

Meanwhile, George was invalided out of the Seaforth Highlanders in 1941, and was joined in the business by his elder brother Gordon, a banker before the war. Their father John continued to run the business until his death in 1956. Sales had boomed after 1945, and Gordon & MacPhail still had sufficient stocks to feed the market.

For generations single malt whisky had remained a popular drink only within the Scottish Highlands and the north-east. Everyone else drank blends, but trends began to change slowly, and Gordon & MacPhail won accolades for their malts, including a range called Connoisseurs Choice, which was popular for many years. The firm is among those credited with sustaining the single malt through its lean years: it was one of the first to realise the marketing potential of aged whiskies, marketing malts at 10, 12, 15, and even 20 years. The Elgin warehouse still holds casks of whisky distilled nearly 50 years ago. "At one time the distillers thought a whisky was too old and fit only to be poured away after eight years," points out Ian Urquhart.

The company had an important role in its dealings with the independent operators in a sector which became dominated by the big groups such as Distillers. For Gordon & MacPhail bottled, packaged, and marketed many malts and blends on behalf of the smaller distillers. It has sold its own whisky liqueur, Spey Cast, complete with a virtually unchanged label, since 1896. Today's South Street store was described recently as " a shrine for whisky lovers" by one London newspaper.

George Urquhart moved headquarters to the present Boroughbriggs Road site during the 1960s. Over the next 25 years, his children joined the company and worked their way up through the management ranks to join the board. New export markets were found in Japan, Canada, Europe, Singapore, Malaysia, New Zealand, and Hong Kong. The collapse of Soviet communism opened the doors in eastern Europe, first of all in Estonia.

The company now employs 110 staff, and holds 5,000 casks of whisky drawn from dozens of small distilleries. Although the grocery wholesale business had sustained the firm during those frequent lean years for whisky, the massive growth of the supermarket chains hit the British independent grocery trade badly. That forced Gordon & MacPhail to retrench and concentrate on the licensed trade, supplying whisky, spirits and wine throughout the country. A new administrative block, named "George House" after the company chairman, is home to a computerised sales and distribution centre. "We have had to move with the times," remarks Ian, who trained in

Harrods food hall before returning to join the family firm. "The pattern of trade has changed quite drastically over the years."

George Urquhart remains chairman at 77, having wound down his involvement gradually since he was 60. He enjoyed his lengthy period in day to day charge of the business, and especially the opportunities for foreign travel, meeting customers and potential buyers. Ian, who became managing director in 1993 after working through all the departments of the company, remembers that his father would be abroad for up to three months at a time on such trips.

"Family businesses tend to be in the value added products, not the mainstream," says Ian. "They tend to work at the expensive end of the market, but they continue to be able to sell on quality.

"As an independent company we can do things which we could not really do as part of a large organisation."

The family kept the Gordon & MacPhail name, even though the two founders' direct involvement ended more than 80 years ago, because it was so well established in the trade. But the fact is that, albeit on solid foundations, the Urquharts built the company and retained its independence when many of its competitors either sold out or went to the wall.

The decision to acquire the Benromach distillery was taken before Gordon & MacPhail's centenary year of 1995. It represents a quite romantic completion of the circle for the company.

The distillery was founded in 1898, built deliberately beside a railway junction at Forres to help ease distribution. It was designed by an Elgin architect, Charles Doig, for two businessmen, a Mr MacCallum, who owned a distillery in Campbeltown, Argyll, and a Leith spirits broker called Mr Brickman. He was brought down by the "Pattison Crash", and MacCallum sold out to a London firm, Eustace Jameson, which began distilling operations in 1909. It changed hands several times before being acquired by Distillers in 1953, closing down 30 years later.

The acquisition of their own distillery, more than a century after the company's founding, would bring a smile to the man who brought it all about and established Gordon & MacPhail so successfully as a whisky trader. John Urquhart will be watching benignly as the first "new" bottles of Benromach malt hit the grocery shelves. His successors intend the move to be a signal of their determination to remain independent and pass his legacy to the next generation when it assumes charge of this very typical Speyside business.

CHAPTER FOUR

The Do It Yourself Millionaire

Gerard Eadie frowns as he considers the question about whether he would ever visit a customer's house at the wheel of his Bentley. Finally he concludes that yes, he probably could do so today, without fear of facing the familiar brick-bats aimed at Scotland's enterprise class.

His reasoning? "They would probably expect it now. We are a well known company. They know we are successful. And I think attitudes have changed a bit these days. I would not have done it in the past."

The company he refers to as "we" is of course the Fife-based double-glazing company C. R. Smith. And anyone who comes across either the company or the man would know that the "we" in question is really Eadie himself. As 100 per cent owner, Gerard Eadie built this company from a one-horse provincial glazing business to a mini-giant in the British market. He had plenty of help from long-standing employees, including his two brothers, but this company depends on his own single-minded approach to business.

Eadie has been described variously as a Scottish whizz-kid, as a hard-driving autocrat, and - to the public at least - remembered as the first and only businessman to recognise the merit of having his company's name emblazoned across the shirts of both Rangers and Celtic football teams. That was a risk that other Scottish companies had spurned, and one which the clubs themselves thought would never happen. It took an audacious decision from a man who professes at first to know "very little" about football, before launching into a lengthy and well-informed discussion regarding the commercial fortunes of Celtic, on whose shirts the C. R. Smith logo remains. Typically, he attributes the original idea to take on the proposal to one of his brothers.

Eadie himself is a complex individual who believes in keeping his business philosophy simple. His competitors, his detractors, and a few former employees have made the mistake of under-estimating his real strength, which is an innate understanding of business basics coupled with a fearsome determination to succeed. The fact is that while the man's philosophy may be simple, his unschooled business manner is sophisticated enough to have survived the best and worst swings of the volatile housing and home improvement markets over the last 25 years.

Today Eadie administers a company which turns over £28m in a bad year, as well as overseeing Greenock-based Blair Joinery, which he bought from receivership and helped to turn around. The two companies employ around 1,000 people. His interests are broad, encompassing Celtic, his boyhood passion of racing cycling, and a falconry school in which he has invested his own money and a great deal of his time during recent years. At 44, Eadie admits: "I get bored easily. I need excitement. Sometimes you wake up and there is a crisis on the horizon, and even though it is something you would rather not have, you become motivated. I need action, I need success to keep me going."

There is a typical example of Eadie's commercial resolve. One Friday morning back in June 1987, having turned in late after one of his routine late-night conversations with a sales manager, he received a 6am call to tell him that his company's newly-completed headquarters in Dunfermline was burning down. An electrical fault destroyed the entire building: Eadie could see the flames from four miles away as he drove hurriedly to the scene.

Some would have been tempted to book a holiday and wait for the insurance company to send a cheque. But selling is the lifeblood of C.R. Smith, and business was booming during that period of the 1980s. Eadie was determined that no business would be lost as a result of the blaze. Later that morning he, his brothers George and Hugh, and production director Ed Hood, created an ad hoc crisis management team. Their aim seemed impossible, but in a single weekend, temporary telephone lines were hired from BT, the computer system was moved to the staff canteen, and architects called in to set up a new, temporary home.

By the following Monday, fewer than 72 hours after the last firefighter left the scene, power had been restored, and 14 Portacabins installed in the car park, providing a new sales centre, some of them having arrived from distant parts of Scotland with police escorts. For good measure, on the Saturday evening a large barbecue and mobile disco was set up, since C.R. Smith had sponsored that weekend's Dunfermline half marathon, and had planned a party to coincide.

At any one time C.R. Smith was handling 4,000 orders. Eadie simply could not afford any delay. The company's "Portacabin City" lasted for more than six months, until the HQ was rebuilt, and turnover actually increased. Ironically, Eadie had been telling one senior colleague the day before the blaze that "things were getting a bit dull". His action in a crisis brought out his basic instinct to organise, succeed and thrive.

There are few clues from his upbringing which might explain just what drives Gerard Eadie. He was brought up in west Fife by his Lanarkshire-born parents, Anne Therese from Shotts, and Hugh from Caldercruix, who died when Gerard, the eldest of four children, was just 19. He attributes his personal drive to his mother: "She had all of us convinced that we were different in some way. She pushed us on, not at school in my case because that was a lost cause. But she was a very strong influence."

Soon after leaving St. Columba's secondary in Cowdenbeath (where his mother taught), Gerard served his apprenticeship as a glazier with Fife County Council. He looks back on that period now and realises that the choice of trade - which may have seemed deliberate given his decision to start up business in the same field - made no real difference to his eventual career, in that he expected he would be successful in whichever area of commerce he chose. His ambition far outstripped any concern about what he would actually end up doing: in fact his teenage dream had been to move to the Continent and try his hand at cycle-racing for money. "It was my passion. I read that two cyclists I admired were market gardeners, so first I got into the Elmwood horticultural school in Cupar. So if I had not gone into glazing I probably would have opened garden centres for example.

"My idea was that I would head for the Continent at 20, and maybe come back and start something at 30. I was 16 and impressionable. My Dad used to say 'the trouble with you is that once you get the bug for something nothing else matters'. That is probably true, but then that attitude has helped me too."

Before his miner father died prematurely, Gerard had begun his "apprenticeship" in self-employment already. One day he found himself taking a break in a hut along with a glazier at Glenwood, near the mining village of Ballingray. The housing scheme was in a "bad area", and its bleak townscape betrayed all the familiar depressing symptoms of vandalism and social decline. "The caretaker asked if I would repair some windows. There were two of us, and I had barely learned how to do the basics of cutting glass and putting it in properly. The other guy wasn't interested, so I went up and measured the windows and just guessed a price."

Gerard's father loaned him the necessary £5 and even went along to a sleepy small local glazing supplier, C. R. Smith, to buy the glass for him. "I was worried sick I wouldn't be able to give my Dad back the £5. I took my brother George, who was still at school, and he helped me do the windows one Saturday morning. When we had fixed everything the old guy came out and found the treasurer, and they gave me £30. We thought we had won the pools."

Until then, Gerard still had dreams of competing in the European cycling circuit. Instead, approaching 20, he set up in business on his own, helped by a further £50 loan from his mother. As he drove round the Cowdenbeath and Dunfermline areas fixing glass, Mrs Eadie and younger sister Rosemary fielded telephone calls for him at home. His long standing friend and an early customer, construction company operator John Muir, reminds Eadie that "he would call at night to ask me to do windows in his houses, and that I would always leave my Mum and Rosemary to take the calls and get the flak!"

Gerard was about to make a key discovery which was to set him fatefully on the road to success, and that was the huge growth in double glazing and home improvements which was looming in the mid 1970s. He would find out soon that the key to success would come from learning the mysterious arts of sales and marketing, and not from being a glazier running a simple back street one-man business. He realised he had to look further afield for sales, and add value to his service in order to compete with national firms, steering ahead of every other jobbing tradesman in the area. An entrepreneur was evolving.

"At the time I just kept going. I would use whatever labour I could find. Say I was doing a window in a shop on the High Street. Some of these panes would take 10 men to lift, so I would rope in some old men who were passing, or anyone I knew who was not working, or my brothers.

"The first few months went fine, and then the holidays came and it became quiet. Looking back, I was thinking ahead even then. I think a lot of people go into business and they are good at what they do, but they never think of sales, they never try and learn that little extra that helps build a business."

The breakthrough, in terms of realising what his true potential might be, came when Eadie repaired a customer's windows for £30. The man had wanted the job done in a hurry, and wrote a letter of thanks, praising Eadie for the quality of work. Months later he noticed the same customer had had completely new double-glazing fitted by a national supplier. "That would have cost him £3,000, and here I was doing £30 jobs. That is when I started to look around. And I realised that you needed to sell."

He approached a friendly Bert Smith, owner of C. R. Smith, a 60 year old business founded by the owner's grandfather and handed down by his father, but not one which Smith himself enjoyed running. Turnover was just £400 a week, and Bert wanted out. He sold to the younger man for £2200: half for the business, and half for its Olivetti cash machine. "In those days I thought it was important to tell people to buy from a local company - not something I would say now of course! We were local in Dunfermline, but Bert moved to open another shop in Alloa and let us use the address, which allowed us to be 'local' in Alloa and Stirling as well."

It was 1976. While small-timers like Eadie were chasing repair work, the new British giants like Everest were becoming famous because of their national TV advertising campaigns. Britain's housing stock, both public and private, was falling into disrepair long after the building booms of before and after the Second World War. "Do it Yourself" was becoming fashionable, and home improvements were fuelling bank lending. Everest had used a series of celebrated ads featuring the TV personality Ted Moult, who would drop a feather down the seal of a double-glazed unit in order to "prove" that it shut out all draughts. Teams of salesmen were touring the housing estates selling new double-glazed windows, often on credit. Eadie realised he had to enter the market if he was to succeed at all.

Had he stopped to take stock, Eadie might have contemplated the fact that he was the raw epitome of everything that resides in the business text-books. A young working-class man with few educational qualifications, he set out to realise his ambitions by hard work and an unusually high level of self-reliance. He had no start-up cash - apart from those two tiny loans from his parents - and knew that he must finance growth from business income rather than by bank overdraft.

And he knew that to develop further, he had to identify new market gaps, and equip his business in order to tackle them seriously. The apprentice glazier had become tradesman, salesman, employer, and managing director in quick succession. Still in his early twenties, he had achieved that much without reference to his peers, without a supportive group of professional advisers, and with no educational achievement. His was raw entrepreneurism.

Many firms the size of C .R. Smith today would have spent comparative fortunes on management consultancy over the years, and their boards would include several non-executive directors and senior managers. Apart from his mother's £50, Eadie has had just one loan, when the Scottish Development Agency and the investment company 3i offered £140,000 between them, towards the cost of completion of his company headquarters in Dunfermline. When 3i suggested that they might take equity as part of the deal, Eadie retorted that he would rather refuse their money. They invested anyway.

Instead of the textbook, Eadie ran his business by instinct. Looking back today, he believes he would have done a few things differently. Clearly, he lacked a business father figure: the advice of an experienced business "friend" has been invaluable to other self-starters. Yet even he cannot find an answer as to whether, if things had gone differently, they might have led to success in any case: perhaps his untutored approach was exactly what C. R. Smith needed.

He admits his approach at first was extremely raw. "I asked a couple of guys, salesmen that I had come across, if they had any ideas about how I should get into this. One of them told me 'what you need is a suit'. He meant that to sell double-glazing, what you needed was a suit, a briefcase, and a window. This guy had a suit and a pair of white sandshoes - not someone you would take on these days."

Another early recruit exited when Gerard's then girlfriend and later wife, Rhona, spotted his picture on a wanted poster while visiting a local police station with a community group. "My recruitment procedure back then was like that. Someone was a 'salesman' because his father had been, even though he never would be. It was all hit and miss," recalls a rueful Eadie.

The glazing sector, about to explode commercially, was still in its infancy. Apart from the major groups like Everest, few people actually knew the potential of the business. Although most business was to be had in the private market, the public sector was soon to provide a new stream of business for the home improvement giants, under the Conservative Government's "right to buy" scheme for council housing which was launched in 1980. That came later: Eadie admits cheerfully that during his fledgling days of the mid 1970s, his only real motivation was in making some money: he knew very little about the different types of approach needed in this sector. But he was a quick learner.

"At first I would just buy aluminium windows from someone else, and have them fitted. The first job was in Burntisland. I bought the windows in Leith, and I was a nervous wreck about it, but when I got there the joiner said everything had gone OK. On my way back to pick up my mother in Dunfermline I took a back road and this little Austin A40 passed me on a corner. I went right off the road and smashed my Vauxhall VX/490 into a telegraph pole: my mind was elsewhere.

"It was just like that. I travelled a great deal, and did a lot of my thinking then. I kept moving round thinking about what I should do next."

Marketing was a basic necessity which Eadie had understood at an early stage, although his had been an unsophisticated approach. He hired an Edinburgh graphics' artist to come up with what was to evolve into the now-familiar blue and white company logo, reasoning that his firm needed an identity around its home area. "I had three or four vans and two salesmen on the road. The salesmen had a Morris Ital and an Austin Maxi. I had an Escort RS2000, and all the cars were different colours. Most local builders would stick those awful little magnetic letters on their vans, and I knew I needed something better than that.

"The salesmen said they would leave if I put the blue stripe down their cars. The Ital was yellow and the Maxi was maroon. I think these guys had told their pals they had company cars, and they did not want the signs all over them. So my entire sales force was going to leave, which made me stop to think. But I did it anyway."

Eadie would not have used the term "raising awareness" when he decided on that blue stripe. But he knew what he wanted, and that was to make his firm much better known within its local market. The blue and white logo was such a success that it inspired other companies to follow suit and opt for a distinctive "branding" of their own vehicle fleets, most notably in the case of Wiseman Dairies.

Again working on instinct, Eadie began to dabble with advertising in the local Dunfermline Press. With £2,000 in the bank, he booked four weekly ads at £500 each. "On the fifth week I still had nothing to show for it. And then a job for £2,000 worth of windows came in from Alloa. I knew then it was worth it. Looking back, if I had been an accountant I probably would have stopped spending the money long before that job came in."

Eadie was beginning to attract attention. And publicity. Over the next few years, his C. R. Smith vans were travelling further afield for work, and his sales force was growing steadily. He became accustomed to wearing a suit, and had given up cutting glass many moons beforehand. His brothers George and Hugh had joined the management. Sales were reaching £8m a year. One day Gerard took a surprising call from Glasgow -based public relations' consultant Michael Murphy.

"He told me there was an opportunity to sponsor both Rangers and Celtic. It was half a million pounds to have both clubs for three years. That was a good deal, but not if you did not have that kind of money," remembers Eadie.

This was 1984. Celtic and Rangers, although by far the largest clubs in Scottish football, were not commercially healthy. Both were owned and run by people who had inherited the business, some of whom lacked the dedication to build success. Onfield, the clubs were undergoing an indifferent period: during the early 1980s Scottish football had been dominated by Aberdeen, and to a lesser extent Dundee United, both of whom appeared then to have broken the stranglehold enjoyed by the "Old Firm" for so many years. In the modern situation where hard-nosed businessmen like David Murray and Fergus McCann have entered the scene it would seem incredible to think that the Old Firm were the only Premier League clubs not to have a sponsor's name festooned on their players' jerseys.

Eadie, grappling in the market place with UK giants like Everest and Coldshield, had been acutely aware of the need to up the ante in terms of public recognition: he was applying the same basic logic which had prompted him to paint his vans the same colour soon after starting up in Dunfermline. Now C.R. Smith had begun to strike out further afield. The company boss used to stop in small Scottish towns wherever he travelled, and knock doors to ask the inhabitants if they had ever heard of C. R. Smith. Three months before

Murphy's call, the company had spent a small fortune on its first TV advertising campaign: the response had been unconvincing so far. Eadie wanted results, reasoning that business would come more easily if Scottish customers perceived C. R. Smith to be an important national operation.

"I knew nothing about football. I could not tell you anything about the League or the Scottish Cup, and I did not understand where Celtic and Rangers were placed. But my brother George was a football player and a fan, and he saw the potential.

"John Paton of Rangers was fine to get along with, even though we were Catholics (the club's Protestant affiliations were still quite notorious then, long before its sensational signing of the Catholic-born player Maurice Johnston). Desmond White, the Celtic chairman saw us as an encumbrance: he would rather there was nothing on the jerseys and that we were not there. But Jack McGinn got things done for us at Celtic. It really is amazing when you look back on it - neither of these clubs had a sponsor. I do not think they had even thought about it."

The deal went through, making a little bit of history, and earning massive publicity. Given the deep-seated rivalry of the two Glasgow clubs and their supporters, the boldness of the deal was met with amazement, and a certain admiration. There is no doubt the sponsorship was a commercial risk, not least because of the large sum of cash involved. But next time he found himself in the Speyside town of Keith, Eadie met an elderly woman who had heard all about the company.

Eadie knew that he had hit on something worthwhile: the football clubs' sponsorship helped push national recognition up to 90 per cent in one survey. The popular Scottish comedian Andy Cameron had a regular sketch in his TV show where he wore a football top that was half-Celtic and half-Rangers - with C. R. Smith's logo across the centre; Eadie himself popped up in business press photographs wearing one of the strips. The company may never have been fashionable beforehand, but it was quickly becoming famous.

"I think the TV ads would have worked for us eventually. We had been doubling our turnover each year. But the football deal catapulted us into people's minds much more forcefully. It was instant," points out Eadie. The timing was particularly helpful because of the growing spate of council house sales across Scotland. People no longer had to wait for their local authority to fix a window. After buying, usually at a large discount, the tenants turned owner-occupiers would begin invariably to "do up" their homes. Double glazing was a priority. And there was still tax relief on home improvements, a concession which survived until the late 1980s.

It was around this time that Eadie began to attract a lot of personal publicity, including a TV documentary which portrayed him as one of a new breed of whizz-kids in Scotland. He was compared often to the similarly-aged David

Murray, who was building a substantial metals' distribution and property management business in Edinburgh and only toying then with the idea of investing in sport, having already run a basketball team. Eadie was filmed being chauffeured around in his Bentley, which was equipped with telephone and fax machine: a rare spectacle in those days. He had a special turntable built in the office garage at Dunfermline HQ so that he need never have to reverse the car. Eadie was perceived as a Thatcherite "Champagne Charlie" who enjoyed the high life, an image far removed from reality. Eadie is as down to earth today as he was when he cycled freely around west Fife dreaming of winning the Tour de France back in his teens.

What he had done was work extraordinarily hard, and to expect similar effort from his colleagues and staff. He was tough, and tough-minded, and if anything his public persona was that of a gruff, bad tempered businessman. Although he has been compared repeatedly with Murray, the two are very different personalities.

Today Eadie still owns his Ferrari - now more than10 years old - and a Bentley, and lives with his wife, two sons and daughter on a large property in Kinross-shire. His clothes come from Versace, and his children go to private school. Eadie is comfortably off, but today he does not give the impression of a man who works just for the money. He cycles often to work, and goes about his daily business in a less-flashy Range Rover.

As a loner, and one who is absorbed deeply in his business, Eadie can be difficult with strangers. When I first met him one lunchtime in his office suite at Dunfermline he stared morosely into his soup before asking: "You must vote Labour, eh? All journalists are against the Conservatives aren't they?"

His mood soon mellowed. Significantly, this incident followed soon after a rather bizarre row over trade union recognition within C. R. Smith in 1986, and a brief strike which had seriously strained Eadie's relationship with Dunfermline's two Labour MPs at the time, Gordon Brown and Dick Douglas. Eadie, long used to positive publicity, was being criticised in the press for his resistance to the overtures of the T&GWU.

The dispute appears with hindsight to have resulted from a misunderstanding. The company planned to reorganise itself so that its joiners cum salesmen in Fife would work from local depots, the idea being that they would be physically closer to their customers. The men did not accept Eadie's assurance that they would not lose income as a result. They joined the union and went on strike, soon to be joined by production workers.

Eadie has since blamed the dispute on a weak communications policy, and introduced regular staff briefings, as well as familiar steps such as a company newsletter and consultative committees. The experience fits in with the image of a man who has had to learn the more sophisticated aspects to business as he has gone along.

He made typically blunt public statements during the strike, setting ultimatums on contracts and insisting that his company would not recognise the union, which had approached the matter quite aggressively too. Eadie's stance drew criticism from the local Labour MPs, and particularly Dick Douglas.

The MP participated in the following year's Dunfermline half marathon but blocked out the name of the race sponsor, C. R. Smith, on his shirt. Eadie took this personally, and erected 10 giant bill posters locally, showing older pictures of Douglas happily posing in company outfits, including that celebrated "Old Firm" strip. The poster challenged him: "Make Your Mind Up, Dick!" Douglas threatened court action, and both men held press conferences to get their point across. The spat blew over quickly, but shows that Eadie is both sensitive about his company's image, and determined to fight his corner whenever external forces attack the operation. He probably calculated, rightly, that the row might also win the company some free publicity, which it did.

So in the late 1980s Eadie could be abrasive at first encounter. But he had enjoyed, or endured, a great deal of publicity by then. And clearly he decided to step out of the limelight when recession began in 1989, concentrating instead on the demands of a business: he marketed C.R. Smith rather than himself. A chance meeting some time later revealed a much different Gerard Eadie, one who could sit for hours drinking tea and discussing football, business affairs, and only a little politics. He was wooed at one time by the Conservatives, especially by figures like the Edinburgh financier Peter de Vink, who ran a Tory Party business group. But, whatever his private politics, Eadie is not too interested in becoming actively involved. This is not unusual among single-minded businessmen who see politics as an unnecessary distraction.

He was interviewed twice for this book. On the first occasion he had to cut things short because of the arrival of a local photographer, Lesley Donald, who wanted a picture for the Herald newspaper. It appeared the following day, Eadie in cycling gear astride his bike, pictured as a reflection on the door-panel of his beloved but not often driven Ferrari Testarossa.

At a second meeting in a Glasgow hotel, his conversation was punctuated by frequent calls from the office and from business associates. He dealt with each call quickly, returning to his topic without a break in concentration, picking up exactly where he had left off, which is an unusual feat.

Having summoned a manager from Blair Joinery to drive to Glasgow from Greenock, he asked the man to wait at another table until his boss's interview was finished. That took another hour. Eadie jumps enthusiastically from one subject to another, and is little interested in the finer details of anything outside his business affairs. It can be difficult at times to do justice to a typical conversation with Eadie in print, as his style of speech is very natural, and moves from one theme to another very quickly.

A good example of his "do it yourself" approach to business administration comes with C. R. Smith's early move into manufacturing. Today, the company runs a high-tech assembly operation in Cowdenbeath, where windows, doors and conservatories are custom-built to customer specification by computer-controlled machines.

But the first move into making double-glazed units took place in Dunfermline, on the site which is now head office. Eadie rented the premises from his local authority, and started looking around to find out the best means of manufacture, there being several methods available. "I would get the machine manufacturers in and ask them, picking up information. They were salesmen telling you different ways to make the units, so I just listened to them all and started to decide how to do it.

"You would listen to the first guy talking about how to cut the glass by machine, and how to optimise it and so on. And that would sound pretty good. But then somebody else would come in and tell you a different way of doing it. I just went on like that, picking up details before I decided what to do."

He admits that he knew nothing about production itself, nor anything about who to recruit for such specialised work. His first factory manager was a former Navy marine engineer - "I thought 'well that's near enough, some sort of engineer'," he jokes - and together they muddled through. Later Eadie recruited Brian Coyne, a former Timex factory manager with greater experience of production methods. "It is all about recruiting the right people. There is no science to it. No matter how smart you are you will never get it right with people, and you'll never set anything up if you do not just try things out." Today the Cowdenbeath operation is acknowledged as one of the most efficient in Britain.

Eadie is frank about his youthful failings, reasoning that he learned from each mistake. In answer to a question about whether his naivete might actually have helped him progress, he says: "If you have the type of nature and personality that says that this is what you want to do, and you can see that you need to work things out to be able to do it, then you don't get put off doing things.

"That is multiplied heavily by youth because you have not had that many knocks, and you have plenty of time on your side. But I think as you get older and you have made a few mistakes, and things have got bigger so there are more implications, then you do lose something. Hopefully that is more than compensated for by that stage, because you have a lot more competent people around you."

Eadie has a sign in his own office asking the pointed question "Asset or Overhead?" He has a dry sense of humour, and communicates closely with his sales team. The emphasis is on teamwork, and targets are kept high. Another sign in the humming sales HQ asks simply: "How Many Windows Did You

Sell today?". One employee says of him: "Gerard is just a great man, with a lot of drive. He gets things done."

Brother George, a year younger than Gerard, is group finance director, and Hugh (a year younger again) is in charge of the conservatories' business, a recent innovation which sprang out of the popularity of double-glazing. Gerard's prime day to day concern is sales, although he has senior managers there as well as in manufacturing. "Sales is the bottom line. The person in charge must always pay attention to that."

He is matter of fact about his mistakes: "I went down south and tried to get our product into the DIY stores, which lost me a million quid. Then I tried again and lost another million. I was just sure it was the right idea."

Although his brothers have been involved in the business, Gerard remains the only shareholder: for them to buy in once the company began to grow would have been too expensive. He admits: "Early on I would have found it really difficult to listen to anybody. I did not want anybody to tell me what to do. Looking back, if I had got the right person, someone older, it might have been a good thing." He finds the situation at Blair Joinery, which does have other shareholders, a bank-nominated chairman and a board to which he must answer, "quite a good discipline".

Blair was an ambitious independent company which had invested in state-of-the-art machinery to develop its innovative timber window-frame products. Recession hit hard, and before a return could be found on that latest investment, Blair's headed into receivership. Eadie was uninterested at first, but greatly impressed by the production area, and even though the two companies were in quite different businesses, he saw an opportunity. Blair's recovery has been slow, but the workforce has grown since Eadie acquired the firm in 1991, and recently it celebrated a £1m order to fit out the insurance company Canada Life's HQ in Toronto.

His great pastime of the moment is something that began as a social interest and resulted, inevitably, in a business venture. Lands of Finderlie is a falconry school cum corporate hospitality company. Typically it began on a whim: Eadie had taken up shooting at one stage, but found birds of prey more fascinating than plugging game birds.

Within a few months he had invested thousands of pounds in recruiting bird-handlers and on buying hunting birds. He believes he has spotted a gap in the burgeoning hospitality market. The idea is that a group of guests spend a day out with their hosts, tramping the hills accompanied by hunting dogs, a fleet of four wheel drive vehicles, and the Harris Hawks and Goshawks. Rather than shoot a pheasant, a guest may watch his or her bird chase a rabbit. So far, the idea is catching on, albeit slowly.

He has quickly assembled one of the biggest private collections of birds of prey in Europe. He believes corporate clients will tire of golf or racing outings and opt for falconry as "something different". He has been known to introduce the birds and explain their history himself, rather than leaving it to one of his hired professionals.

Eadie has an unquenchable enthusiasm for everything that attracts his attention. He can be impulsive: his first Ferrari was purchased simply because he had stopped to look at it in a showroom, having had no intention of buying such a fancy car.

An acquaintance tells a typical tale of Eadie's business addiction. In the hills of Kinross, this man was watching the flight of a hawk, majestic in midair, surveying the land below. He glanced down from this picture of rural serenity to observe Eadie standing directly underneath the bird, barking instructions back to base on his mobile phone.

He has not yet thought about the succession. He and Rhona have two boys and a girl, the eldest son being just 16, and at 44 Eadie has no intention of standing down. "I have built up a name. I would like to capitalise on that. I think I have a team of smart people here now, and I would like to develop C. R. Smith as a blue-chip name. Not in terms of becoming a big public company, but as something which people recognise as a good business."

He has no plans to sell out either, having rejected several inquiries from major competitors during recent years. It is very hard to imagine Gerard Eadie working for someone else.

One interesting facet of Eadie is that he had no business role models in his youth, an unusual fact when compared to other high-fliers who started out young. "I think today we have many more young people going into business. People are more ambitious today. Twenty years ago people acted as if all the opportunities were gone.

"Life can be tough in business. But I remember thinking when I was young and in competitive cycling that things were tough. Then I realised they were tough for everyone else in the race. So when we are talking inside the company about tough times, I always think the rest of them, the competition, must be having it tough too."

Gerard Eadie is the ultimate do-it-yourself entrepreneur. He had few role models as he grew up and entered business, and he is unlikely ever to sell out and become a visiting professor somewhere, lecturing up and coming youngsters on the triumphs and tribulations of self employment: his life is dedicated solely to the development of his own business. And his story is a model of success built upon one young man's single-minded and flinty determination to do well.

CHAPTER FIVE

Pint-sized Ambition

T
wo large maps adorn the wall of Alan Wiseman's office headquarters in the one-street hamlet of Nerston, just outside East Kilbride. So far in his company's meteoric growth, there has been little need for the world version, but the Scottish map is now peppered with the Wiseman Dairies' presence, as this unique company races to dominate the milk market.

In business terms the Wiseman brothers' success has been explosive. During the late 1980s, the company emerged from central Scotland's legion of small, local dairies to become a dominant player in a fast-changing market dominated previously by the dairy co-operatives such as the Scottish Milk Marketing Board.

In 15 years to 1995, Wiseman bought 41 rival companies, the most significant being those of Kennerty Farm and the Co-operative Wholesale Society (CWS). In Scottish terms, that is a rate of acquisition outstripped only by longer-established operators such as Lord Macfarlane of Bearsden, who as Norman Macfarlane acquired more than 200 companies for his Glasgow packaging business.

Today Robert Wiseman & Sons is comfortably within the league of Scotland's top 100 companies. In 1992, executive chairman Alan Wiseman spoke wistfully of leaping towards the £100m sales' mark from the current figure of £38m. The target was surpassed within two years, and the company had expanded firmly into the North of England.

Now Wiseman envisages itself as becoming a rival to Yorkshire-based Northern Foods, in terms of size and local influence within its markets. "It is all tremendous fun. To create something and watch it grow really is a marvellous experience," comments Alan Wiseman.

Although their growth is a tribute to their collective determination, the Wisemans are also a creation of de-regulation. The government's effort to strip away market controls in an attempt to create greater competition - fuelled by European Commission concerns about the virtual State monopolies of the milk marketing boards - has resulted in the former "nationalised" type operators facing new, aggressive competition from the private-sector. None has been more aggressive, or more successful, than the Wiseman brothers.

Today Alan and his brothers Robert and Gavin still run the company from the former farmhouse where they grew up helping their father, Robert, run milk deliveries across the then-growing new town of East Kilbride. "I used to come straight home from school and start washing bottles," recalls Alan, who has received both the Scottish Businessman of the Year and Scottish Business Achievement awards in recent years. "We worked very hard organising everything for the men to start their rounds the next morning.

"When they had finished my mother Jean laid on a big breakfast for everyone at the house. We still go round to the house most days for soup at lunchtime."

It may seem a far cry from those humble beginnings to today. The original farmhouse, bought by Robert Wiseman in 1959, has been extended and extended again to serve as headquarters of an operation which spans Scotland and the North of England. Where once there were milk-floats and dairy trucks, the car park includes sports cars and expensive high-spec all-terrain vehicles: the fruits of success for a family whose by-word has been hard labour. The Wiseman's unpretentious "executive suite" of offices has been carved out of the boys' former bedrooms, with a familiar view of Lanarkshire moor land.

A total of 40 people work at HQ, including eight employed in the workshop which services the Wiseman lorry fleet.

Alan, aged 45 and the eldest of five children, is the company's public face. It would be simplistic to describe him as the brains and the public voice of the operation, but if he is, then brother Robert, 40, is the brawn. Commuting large distances each day, Robert operates as a mobile nerve-centre, in charge of everything from negotiating milk deliveries to supervising the day to day details of running a £100m business.

Living in Auchterarder, he splits his week between Aberdeen, Glasgow, and Nerston, driving on his managers either in meetings or by telephone. Where Alan is polished and down-to-earth, Robert is amiable, but in the words of one associate, "he doesn't suffer fools gladly". His older brother describes him as "the powerhouse".

He does not mince words or waste time either. There is little room for sentiment in the modern milk industry, as Robert made clear when the company bought CWS. He said then that the CWS operation in Glasgow's Pollokshields would probably close, so that work could be transferred to Bellshill and another Glasgow plant in Possilpark. The operation closed down within a few months. At least the trade unions who protested at the closure could not complain about a lack of straight talk.

Another brother, Gavin, 38, is the junior member of the management team, heading administration and purchasing. Another key member of management is Jack Buchanan, a boyhood friend who was best man at Alan's wedding and remains distribution director, having joined the company from school. Only one other brother, Colin and the Wisemans' sister Jean are outwith the company, although the family remains close. Even company founder Robert, 80, keeps in touch: as Alan discussed the firm's history one wintry Saturday morning, his father appeared outside to shovel snow from the path.

Robert and his brother John had operated a small 140-acre dairy operation with a herd of Ayrshire cattle, Murray Farm, when East Kilbride Development Corporation began building the new town. "They gave six months' notice to quit to make way for the development, and Dad bought the site here at Nerston," recalls Alan. At that time, with no new town and therefore no by-pass, Nerston straddled the busy road between Glasgow and Strathaven.

The company's growth mirrored that of East Kilbride, the first Scottish new town which proved to be a big attraction for the so-called "Glasgow overspill" families enticed to the Lanarkshire town by new and better housing and the prospect of a job in one of the "new" industries. Families brought up in tenement flats with little or no comforts, or who had been packed off to schemes like Castlemilk immediately after the war, saw the prospect of bringing up their children in houses with internal plumbing and even a back garden as a golden one. East Kilbride grew quickly and, despite early structural problems such as the lack of proper community amenities which bedeviled every new town until the late 1970s, it is judged to be a social and economic success.

Now home to more than 80,000 people, East Kilbride has become a commuter town for Glasgow, and a base for major international manufacturing companies such as the electronics giants Motorola, JVC, and Siemens, and until recently Rolls Royce. Back in the 1960s and early 1970s, the young Alan Wiseman saw the new town as a means to growth for his father's business, which depended heavily on a burgeoning local market.

From the age of 13, Alan returned from Duncanrigg senior secondary school to help out his father's milkmen by washing and filling bottles for the next morning's deliveries. By the time he had left school in 1965, the family operated five runs in the new housing estates of Murray, Calderwood, East Mains, and Greenhills. So far so good, but the business was little different from any other local milk delivery operator: small and independent, but hardly the makings of a national player which must now attend to its shareholders and City analysts with the same enthusiasm as it serves its market.

Alan traces his ambition back to a boyhood visit with sister Jean to an aunt in Cleveland, Ohio. "My uncle John had always told me to visit America. He believed they were 20 years ahead of the rest of us in most things, and thought I would learn things. He even offered to pay for me to go," Alan remembers.

"Of course I did see something that was to have a big impact on us back home. And that was the growth of the supermarkets. People were increasingly buying their milk from the market rather than having it delivered."

He was a young man, but he had worked since childhood and was steeped in the business by the time he left school. As the eldest child he probably felt an added responsibility too. But given his raw youth, Alan spotted the opportunity offered by future trends such as the growth of the supermarkets, shopping malls, and the creation of "urban sprawl" - the development of commuter suburbs and dormitory towns - which began in America but is now a fixed social feature throughout Britain.

Increasingly, people live further away from the corner-shop. They tend to do their shopping weekly, and often by car. Apart from inner-city and intensely-urban areas, the idea of nipping down to a local store for a pint of milk began to diminish during the 1970s, and accelerated with the growth of supermarket chains like Safeway and Asda during the 1980s. As an example, door-to-door deliveries of milk account for less than 12 per cent of the Wiseman business today, compared to the 100 per cent of the company's first 25 or 30 years. So the phenomenal growth of the business has sailed on a raft of social, economic, and regulatory change. The Wiseman brothers have simply applied their personal drive to the trend.

Alan's first important strategy was to become bigger. This was achieved by the simple route: a grassroots version of growth by acquisition. The family realised that those changes in the market meant that money was to be made only by increasing the geographical spread of their distribution network and achieving better economies of scale.

The young entrepreneur travelled around North Lanarkshire looking for opportunities to take over businesses similar to his father's. "I just knocked on the door. We would usually have tried to work out what a business was doing, and forecast where it was going. I remember as an example there was a Mr Twaddle in Wishaw, in his 60s and running things on his own. I went in and negotiated a price. That was typical; the company grew by that method.

"Looking back the amazing thing was that we had no real hiccups. It was a great plan!"

The brothers financed that growth by borrowing, often by living with the threat of personal guarantees hanging over them. Loans were raised for acquisitions, for installing pasteurising machinery, for the move into cartons instead of bottles. All of it was paid for from the increased cash-flow achieved by increasing their share of what was essentially a very "local" market. Expansion was very localised in those days involving moves from beyond East Kilbride to embrace neighbouring towns like Hamilton, Wishaw, and Motherwell. It was only later that the Wisemans' ambitions would spread across Scotland and beyond its border.

There was little fear of failure. "We just knew what we had to do," remarks Alan. This from a man who in his youth had sought also to augment his income by selling newspapers and breeding rabbits.

The business continued to grow, until Wiseman became part of a small group competing with the milk marketing board for dairy farmers' loyalty. Although the board was essentially a co-operative of farmers, Wiseman secured guaranteed supplies by offering contracts whereby the farmer received an extra penny per litre for his milk. The practice was begun by the major dairy companies, and especially cheese and butter manufacturers. At the time, Wiseman's deals were controversial, probably because it implied a challenge to the long-standing and rather cosy set-up involving all of the dairy industry in Scotland.

It was also a signal of what was to come. As full deregulation approached during the early 1990s, the industry faced an enormous shake-out, and there were fears that farmers in the less populous areas of Scotland would suffer. Milk prices threatened to soar as a result of the free market.

The Wisemans had built a new dairy at Motherwell Food Park in Bellshill, less than 10 miles from their Nerston HQ. But they struck out beyond home base, buying up Mackie's of Aberdeen and their major East Coast rival, Kennerty Farm Dairies.

Now they sit as the major rival to the milk marketing board's post-deregulation successors, Scottish Pride and Scottish Milk, a competition so intense that there has even been talk of a Wiseman takeover of Scottish Pride itself: in 1996 the company had confirmed its interest, although at the time of writing that suggestion was being resisted firmly by the Scottish Pride board. In addition the company has established a dairy and distribution centre in Manchester, aiming to snap up supermarket and wholesale business in the North of England. And in 1995 they bought the Co-operative Wholesale Society's Scottish distribution network, which had sales of more than £20m, or 43m litres of milk. Wiseman's move brought them a 37 per cent share of the market, to Scottish Pride's 42 per cent. The Lanarkshire firm has 4.5 per cent of the UK market already.

Much of this latter expansion has been financed via placements of shares on the Stock Exchange, although the family remains the dominant shareholder in the business. "In 1990 we bought a business in England realising we could do the same there as we were doing at home. But to set up in Manchester meant finding £10m, which was too much to borrow. We were looking at buying Kennerty and so we hired a stockbroker and raised £15m."

The Kennerty acquisition was a major step forward in 1994. Wiseman's bought the Mackie's dairy business for £3.1m before targetting the much bigger Kennerty operation in Aberdeen for £8.1m. Formerly "Reith's of Kennerty", a family business whose most famous member was Lord Reith, founder of the BBC, Kennerty was the dominant player in north-east Scotland, and included a big milk processing plant at Tullos in Aberdeen.

Critics once said Wiseman was simply building up the business in order to sell out at a premium. However, the company's structure and growth ambitions suggest that it will remain independent for as long as possible. "The plc board has three directors: Robert, myself, and our finance director Billy Keane (hired from Scottish Pride). The operational board has 12 directors. We are happy with that structure," says Alan. The brothers retain 63 per cent of the company's shares.

"There has always been a determination to build a really strong Scottish dairy company, and that is matched by a determination to keep family control." So far the company has offered 37 per cent of its share holding as equity for fund-raising, in blocks of 25 and 12 per cent, but the brothers seem determined to retain a majority holding, currently 63 per cent, for as long as possible.

Alan Wiseman attributes his company's growth rate, and public recognition, partly to a lesson learned from another leading independent Scottish entrepreneur, Gerard Eadie, owner of the double-glazing giant C.R. Smith in Dunfermline (whose story is told elsewhere in this book).

"We had about 120 vans on the road then, most of them bought second hand. They were a mishmash of colours, partly because we had thought it important then to leave the old company names on the sides, to keep their local identity. So the vans might have been ours, but they would keep the old names like Hopkins of Bishopbriggs or Wilkie of Blantyre," says Alan.

He was among business people to attend a routine seminar, addressed by Eadie and other well-known business figures including Tom Farmer of Kwikfit and David Stephenson of Edinburgh Woollen Mills. "Gerard Eadie said that he used leaflets for marketing, before he realised that his vans could be converted into what he called a 'poster campaign' on wheels," recalls Alan Wiseman.

Eadie had decided on a firm company image, and added distinctive blue and white paint work to his van fleet, making sure that the company's sales office number was displayed prominently. He told the seminar the result had been huge at the time, and without realising it at the time, his example inspired the Wisemans to embark on their boldest marketing move so far.

"I contacted a design company in Glasgow and told them I wanted an identity: it was as simple as that. I remember watching Postman Pat on TV and thinking that when you saw a red van you thought of the Post Office. I wanted something that gave us what C.R. Smith had got with their design, and what the red van did for the PO."

The result was the now famous Jersey cow design. Apart from a green logo bearing the company name, the fleet was daubed in the familiar black and white pattern of a dairy cow, the aim being to improve recognition.

The gimmick worked. Wiseman began to apply the same design to their own products, so that the name was displayed prominently in the supermarkets. "It sounds so simple, but at the time it looked like we were taking a chance. I must admit when I first saw the cow design I almost rejected it," laughs Alan.

He believes that the new identity helped raise consumer awareness of Wiseman, emphasising that it was by now a major player in the market, and that it brought with it a sense of quality. "You could trust our milk," as Alan Wiseman puts it.

Certainly, bulk milk delivery and the corner-shop remain Wiseman's core business. While the firm supplies most of the major supermarkets with their "own brand" milk, customers are just as likely to pick up a Wiseman carton because they know the name well: a big plus point for independent suppliers, especially in markets like Scotland where shoppers often prefer to know that they are buying Scottish produce.

The Wiseman's definitive move into the market came with the opening of the Bellshill dairy in 1989. "We knew we were good enough to get into the supermarket business. And we knew we had to be serious about it. Which means we had to sort out our processing and distribution," points out Wiseman.

The dairy, on Motherwell food park and at the heart of Scotland's transport distribution network, is a model of efficiency. Milk arrives in bulk tankers, and is packaged using the latest technology. The Wiseman fleet reverses its giant refrigerated trucks into specially-designed loading bays, and everyone's daily pinta is sent off across the country. It is a long way from the days of the horse and cart, and the cost savings have helped fuel expansion, especially in the acquisition of more traditional rival businesses like CWS.

"It has been like a snowball gathering momentum. The reason we were buying second-hand vehicles in the old days was that we were strapped for cash. Robert and I had worked on personal guarantees in those days. Many of the companies we were competing with have disappeared. The market has been incredibly competitive for a long time now," points out Alan.

Since de-regulation the company has been at the heart of the debate. Dairy farmers viewed their aggressive approach with suspicion and more than a little fear. There were dire warnings that Wiseman's acquisition race, combined with its direct deals with big farmers in the richer agricultural areas of Scotland would leave the more remote farmers at a disadvantage. The previous regime had been a co-operative which effectively guaranteed trade for everyone, regardless of geographical location.

However the fact of de-regulation has had no such dire effect. Apart from the Scottish giants, there are dozens of local processors continuing to handle milk. Wiseman has simply created a big enough operation to run an efficient business capable of supplying everything from the domestic customer and corner shop, to caterers and the supermarket chains.

It is significant that Wiseman argues that Office of Fair Trading assessments of the market should look at Scotland and the North of England as a market, rather than concentrating on Scotland alone. That indicates that the company wants to become even bigger in Scotland itself, as well as swelling its English operations. The Manchester dairy supplies a broad geographical market which stretches to Birmingham in the south and Grimsby to the east.

Alan Wiseman is more popular with the dairy industry than a few years ago, when he had to address often angry public meetings of farmers who were worried that the company wanted to become a monopoly and grow rich on the back of their hard work.

It was a time for sensitivities. Wiseman received some needling when a BBC farming programme filmed outside his office and farmers noticed his expensive sports car. He now owns a Rolls Royce, and a 400-acre farm near Hamilton, but these are the trappings of success in a long-standing private firm which first floated some of its shares on the Stock Exchange in 1994.

The relationship between three brothers in any business would come under intense pressure normally, but Alan says he remembers only one serious row with Robert (and, perhaps tellingly, declines to give details). They have adhered to a rule common in family businesses that spouses should not become involved. His own wife, Margaret, was a secretary with East Kilbride Development Corporation, and takes no part in the business.

Alan, Robert, and Gavin, are members of the same golf club. Although they live quite far from each other, they socialise regularly. Until recently, all of them played in competitive curling: Robert has reached the Scottish finals on several occasions, and Gavin represented Scotland at junior level. "From the ages of 17 to 40 I played two or three times a week," says Alan. Now all three play golf and lately have taken up shooting.

The family also owns a holiday home near Gleneagles in the Perthshire countryside, purchased, ironically when their great rival, the milk marketing board, bought out the Wisemans' 16 per cent holding in Scottish Pride. They share access but rarely use the property at the same time.

Alan Wiseman reflects on his family's business success, and believes: "There is a desire to build something really significant. The Office of Fair Trading now look at the milk industry as being a north of Britain market. When we bought CWS they looked at the market north of Birmingham. We have 12-14% of that market. I really want to rank alongside a food company as significant as Northern Foods."

But what drives the family onward? Many larger food companies would happily swallow the business and leave the Wisemans even wealthier. But Alan, Robert and Gavin are too young to retire, even if they wanted to.

"It's just they way we are," believes Alan. "And I hate losing money!"

CHAPTER SIX

No Change to the Recipe for Success

The name of Tunnock strikes a chord for many Scottish grown-ups, bringing back memories of childhood when the very thought of a great sticky Tea Cake, or that famous lump of Caramel Log, was enough to see any youngster through a long school day or a weekend outing.

The biscuits are from Lanarkshire, better known in modern history for its coal mines and steel mills, and their eventual painful decline. One of Scotland's industrial heartlands, the nature of its traditional industries may give a clue as to the chocolate laden biscuits which continue to churn out of the Tunnock family's factory in Uddingston.

Hewing coal or ladling molten steel are not skills for the subtlest of hands. And handling a Tunnock's Caramel Wafer - compared to many of its efficiency-driven, designed by committee competitors - is something of a challenge too. For Tunnock's believe in quality and value for money: an ambition fulfilled by their biscuits, which must rank as among the giants of the market.

The company typifies traditional Lanarkshire in many ways. It is owned by a family which is entrenched firmly in the county's history, and whose growth reflects the social and cultural changes witnessed there. Lanarkshire was always a collection of smaller communities, where everyone knew everyone else. The Co-op, the masonic lodge, the miners' clubs provided a social backbone. Companies like Tunnock's, and there were many of them, competed to supply "purveys" for all these groups and organisations in the early days.

The second chairman, Archibald Tunnock, was the man who put Tunnock's on the map, beating his "purvey" competitors, moving into the chocolate biscuit business, and launching a fleet of brightly painted Tunnock's vans partly in order to raise the company's profile beyond its home base.

Archibald was a County Councillor and a Justice of the Peace: a typical example of a self-made but community minded local businessman. He once got lost in a police station after arriving to hear a local case, and accidentally locked himself in the station cell. It is said that it took a considerable time for the police to accept his story and release him: remarkable in such a small place as Lanarkshire.

And while Tunnock laid on meals or sold biscuits to organisations which included those Lanarkshire miners and steel workers, it also employed many of their wives and daughters. The Tunnock's workforce was a close-knit community in its own right, and continues to be so, something which is accentuated by the firm's family-based management.

The company, founded as a baker's business by Thomas Tunnock in 1890, moved into the biscuit sector in 1946. It had made its name between the wars as the provider of the "purvey" for weddings, conferences, and all sorts of special occasions. Despite its age, the company has been run by only three men: the founder Thomas from 1890 to 1920, his son Archibald from then until his death in 1981, and Boyd Tunnock since then.

This is not a company given to new fangled work methods or endless family strategy meetings. Boyd Tunnock, now 63, starts up the machinery at 8am each day, and is usually still in the factory when the night shift arrives. Between meetings in his office, he dashes around the plant, white-coated and gaunt, greeting his workforce by name wherever he goes. In old age, his father Archibald scooted round the plant aboard an electric tricycle; Boyd relies simply on his own two feet.

Apart from running the company - he and his wife Anne are the only two shareholders - Boyd describes himself jokingly as "chief engineer and head of research and development". The technique of making all those caramel-rich and thickly chocolated biscuits has changed little since their introduction, and the creation of the existing factory building in 1961. Boyd Tunnock, keeper of the famous recipe, is unlikely to vary the mix.

He arrived for his interview at the wheel of a classic 1952 Lagonda sports car, having whisked a couple of foreign suppliers off to lunch. During the meeting he broke off for a detailed discussion with one of his long serving maintenance team concerning the state of a drain at the perimeter of the building. It is hard to imagine the chairman leaving the building at all, given his daily regime, but he does have a keen interest in sailing, having named his Clyde based boat "Lemarac" ("caramel" spelt backwards, naturally).

The reception area of the factory has changed little since its creation. Display cases show whimsical memorabilia from the company history, including handwritten copies of catering orders from the 1920s and 1930s, and wrappers produced in different languages for worldwide markets. The chairman's office, set off with an ancient and faded red carpet, is festooned with similar material, promotional artefacts piled high on chairs, a poster for Uddingston Civic Week, a generic poem about the power of positive thinking. An adjoining office door has a smooth hole in one of its sides, having for years banged against the same piece of furniture whenever it was opened. This is not a company which believes in frittering its healthy profits on fancy overheads.

Most importantly, lying in the same office, and the only hint that this is a modern business, is the coming weeks' media schedule booked by Tunnock's' advertising agency in Glasgow. Tunnock's is a big and regular advertiser, well aware of the importance of its brand and competing with much larger companies.

Six hundred people work three shifts in Tunnock's. Between them they produce 100 tons of caramel and 90 tons of specially mixed chocolate each week. That mass of sweet-tasting mix is combined with a further 50 tons of flour, the whole thing producing more than four million Caramel Wafer biscuits and three million Tea Cakes. "Individually wrapped," points out Boyd. He could talk happily for hours about the intricacies of "enrobing" a naked Tea Cake in chocolate. For good measure, he has been known to service and repair the machines which carry out the task: on the day he was interviewed he and four engineers had been grappling with one of the wrapping machines.

Yet it would be a mistake to dismiss Tunnock's as just an old-fashioned family business. Its annual sales are more than £20m, and its products appear to remain as popular as they ever were, especially in sweet-toothed Scotland. Takeover inquiries have averaged half a dozen each year for many years. "I would be disappointed not to get a few. I just tell my secretary to reply with just the usual letter, 'NIMT' meaning 'no interest meantime'. Why would I want to sell out? What would I do?" Boyd Tunnock's "hands on" policy may seem archaic in modern industrial terms, but it continues to work well for a firm which still lodged its massive daily takings in old book ledgers until computers were introduced just a few years ago.

Boyd, whose brother Thomas was forced to retire through ill-health many years ago, is joined by his daughters Karen as personnel manager and Fiona in charge of export sales. Karen's husband, Fergus Loudon, is Scottish sales manager. There are other children - and grandchildren -too, yet Boyd and Anne remain the only shareholders, signalling that the chairman expects to carry on with the company for many years, just as his father did before him. Archibald was still in charge nominally at the time of his death at the age of 86, although Boyd and Tom were running a large part of the operation for many years before then. "My father was a businessman to his finger tips. He worked here right up to four days before his death, and he even died on Fair Friday (a local holiday) so it didn't affect things too much." reflects Boyd, apparently only half-joking.

Archibald "Archie" Tunnock was a minor legend in Scottish commercial circles. He enjoyed frequent publicity, and was pictured often standing before his Rolls Royce car, with its registration number AT 12. Although he worked right up until his death, both Tom and Boyd had a very active involvement, the elder Tom having played a big part in the company's expansion during the 1960s. Meanwhile, the old man had free time to develop virtually a mini-zoo at his Uddingston mansion, replete with corgi dogs, livestock, and a wide variety of birds, including pheasants, peacocks, and budgerigars: lots of them.

"I don't think the same way my father did in many ways," says Boyd. "But he believed very strongly in hard work and good, simple management. You have to really want to be in business, to want it to continue, and to make money. I do not think of the long term, and I never think of selling out."

He delights in telling the tale of a recent visitor, an engineer, who mentioned that his 96-year-old mother had had her wedding purvey laid on by Tunnock's in 1940. "I looked up the records and found all the details, which I photocopied for him, with all the details about how many were at the wedding, how many steak pie teas we supplied, and the wedding cake itself. He was absolutely delighted: in this life it is all the wee things that count."

Boyd entered the business at 15 in 1946, spending five years at night school learning the crafts of baking. He and another young lad, Archie Fleming, were awarded the Tunnock Medal by his father after tying in the bread-making section with 140 and a half points each. Boyd remembers such details with relish.

National Service followed, and Boyd joined the catering corps, training at Aldershot. He emerged as a Cook Sergeant and rejoined the family business, where his older brother Tom was already making his mark. By 1952 the transformation from bakery to biscuit manufacturer went into full swing for Tunnock's with their introduction of the Caramel Wafer. Sales soared, manufacturing activities increased with the construction of a new factory - virtually unchanged today - nine years later. Tunnock, the Lanarkshire purvey provider for Masonic events and wedding parties, quickly became a nationally recognised name in the highly competitive British biscuit market.

"The great thing about the Caramel Wafer is that it is half-sweet, half-biscuit. Other companies followed with things like the Twix, based also on caramel, which is the most popular sweet taste in biscuits," says Boyd. "Our strength is basically that we are different. I mean, I could go out tomorrow and buy a machine for making digestive biscuits, but I would not sell them because McVitie have the name for them. The same goes for us.

"You need something different, something which has added value and is 'multi-process': make a wafer, boil the caramel, put the two together, let it wait then cover it in chocolate and wrap it. You cannot beat the old head who knows just when the caramel is soft and so on."

A large part of Tunnock's' customer base includes the major supermarket chains, although the company now exports more than 20 per cent of its product, which is particularly popular in the Middle East and south east Asia. "You really have to be supplying the big boys (the supermarkets) these days, or you can forget it. But we do not do 'own label' for them: everything we make is all in our own name."

The original Thomas Tunnock was the son ι f a stone mason who served an apprenticeship as a baker. He bought another business for the princely sum of £80, and began making shortbread and catering for picnics and excursions. Soon he opened a tea room in Uddingston's Bellshill Road, and built up his business until the onset of war in 1914.

By the end of the war Thomas's health became poor, and he died suddenly while still in his early 50s. Son Archibald arrived at Glasgow's Central Station after being demobbed from military service to be told of his father's death: he returned home to reopen the family business. By 1924 he opened a new tea room in the town's Main Street, and expanded the catering business in a very competitive market. It thrived until the second war.

With rationing nearing its end, Tunnock realised he could expand, and did so, building a factory in Old Mill Road, and launching his biscuit lines, realising that he needed a strong brand identity to compete in the new and fast-growing national market. The Caramel Wafer provided the answer: the wafer component is still made using the secret formula devised nearly half a century ago, and which is still kept private by Boyd today.

Archibald Tunnock's knack was in realising the potential of mechanisation. The business grew rapidly as a result. His sons had entered the business, but would work very lengthy "apprenticeships" because their father had no intention of standing down. He had a knack too for marketing: the biscuit packaging was bright and garish, using red and gold to some effect, to the extent that today's wrappings are little changed.

Scotland's famous sweet tooth was to be served by Tunnock's products for many years, and the company began to "export" to England and abroad, especially to the Middle East, where caramel is especially popular. Archie knew how to grab attention: he once offered a new Ford car and hundreds of pounds in prizes to members of the public who invented new names for his biscuits. The company's archives are packed with newspaper interviews and photographs of the chairman: he was one of the new wave of business celebrities, like Hugh, later Lord, Fraser and others who made their fortunes as Britain struggled out of post-war austerity and began to rebuild its economy.

In 1975, his staff commissioned a special flag for the chairman's 80th birthday. He still had no immediate intention of retiring however, although his sons were by then holding senior positions within the operation.

The independent spirit is clearly inherited by Boyd. By modern standards, the company appears to be run along slightly eccentric lines. Yet it continues to thrive. Part of the success lies with the Tunnock "formula", which includes thick wafer and a very rich chocolate mix. It is claimed that Tunnock's biscuits are less likely to melt within the wrapper in hot climates, something which may explain their popularity overseas.

The company is fiercely proud of the fact that it has always been able to fund new investment or expansion from within its own resources: a common sentiment across the family business sector. There is no dilution of equity beyond the chairman and his wife, and no borrowing or bank overdraft. On meeting a new local bank manager who had the impertinence to inquire about the company's accounts a few years ago, Boyd is said to have responded: "I lend you money. When I come to you to borrow money, you can see my books!"

The factory is close-knit. Several generations of many families have worked in the Uddingston plant. Managers are on first-name terms with most people on the production-lines. In recent years, a greater effort has been made to manage the company's finances, introduce new technology, and to meet new manufacturing standards. Product quality has never been an issue with Tunnock, which could claim records in cramming ingredients between its wrappers.

"We do not spend our time in pointless meetings or closeted in corners somewhere in an office-block," says one Tunnock's manager. "Boyd is tireless. He never stops, and he keeps everything he needs in his head. There is a great feeling of involvement."

And yet, and yet. Questions remain about the succession. Does Boyd intend to carry on like his father, and work into his 70s or even 80s? Daughter Karen became personnel manager in 1990, and Fiona's appointment in charge of export sales may be significant. The company is switching that operation from London back to a purpose built office block in Uddingston.

Boyd Tunnock does not discuss this. He speaks of his admiration of the Scots-born US steel magnate Andrew Carnegie, and jokes that he has recently read a book on "how to make friends and influence people": in practice, something Boyd has attempted to do throughout his working life.

"The important thing in a business like this is to get people to gel together. Even in family companies you get people pulling against each other.. You need to mediate," he adds.

"I lead by the Indian chief method. One person has to be in charge. It is not the modern technology method but it seems to work. My other rule is that 'a smile works wonders'."

And what of the future? "We are looking at new markets export-wise, and we have two or three new products on the back burner. You have to stay on the look out."

With that, Boyd Tunnock is off. The beautiful old sports car parked outside may be reminding him wistfully of his youth, when he won the Scottish Sporting Car Club championship in 1959-60. More importantly, there is the night shift to greet and that blocked drain is still needing attention.

CHAPTER SEVEN

The Irn Bru Dynasty

It is "Made in Scotland" - from girders, of course. And it remains, relentlessly, our "Other National Drink". Barr's Irn-Bru is possibly the ultimate Scottish brand name, and its creators have survived by pushing beyond its borders to establish themselves as Britain's biggest independent soft drinks' manufacturer.

Since the 1960s, when Irn-Bru emerged from the ranks of Scottish soft drinks to lead the field and push into England, the drink has become synonymous with Scottish life. Comedians like Billy Connolly have referred to it as part of their act, and generations have laughed at the increasingly sophisticated use of humour in its television advertising. It even sponsors the Scottish international football squad, although sadly the team has not lived up to the drink in terms of success...so far!

Imitation is the sincerest form of flattery, so when a Dundee-based confectionery firm launched a rival drink a few years ago, it was branded as "Rivets", a clear nod to Irn-Bru's famous "made from girders" campaign. Barr's acknowledged the compliment, but in the ensuing sales battle it promptly flattened its new rival, which was withdrawn hurriedly from the market.

A.G. Barr is now the third biggest soft-drinks' company in Britain, behind the two multinational giants, Coca Cola-Schweppes and Britvic, owned by Bass, whose range includes Robinson's and the UK franchises for Pepsi and Tango. The Glasgow firm's annual sales stand at £110m, and even though it has been a "public" company for more than 30 years, chairman and chief executive Robin Barr, a direct descendant of the founding family, believes it is still run very much as it was in the past.

The company's success can be traced to two vital factors in this intensely competitive market: a lifelong determination to increase its share, by aggressive marketing and by the steady acquisition of other British operators; and its usual willingness to move with the times. This company has an iron resolve to match the power-giving claims once made for its flagship product.

As well as owning Irn-Bru and sister brands like Red Kola and American Cream Soda, Barr's is by far the biggest operator in Scotland. It also owns the popular English soft drink brand Tizer, and markets and distributes the French brand Orangina in the UK. Recently it began another joint venture with the New England fruit juice company Welch's. Its products are on the shelves of every British supermarket, jostling for position with the American-owned giants Coke and Pepsi as well as "own brand" colas such as Sainsbury's and the new market intruder, Virgin.

Thirsty British consumers drink nearly nine billion litres of soft drinks each year, a market worth more than £6 billion. Fizzy drinks account for half of that total. This is a cut-throat market, where every innovation - new brand names, new types of bottles, new methods of dispensing the drinks - is seized on by the major competitors. TV and poster advertising, as well as sponsorship, cost millions of pounds each year, and everything is geared towards achieving maximum impact. Coca-Cola sponsored the 1996 Olympics in its home city of Atlanta; Pepsi is "huge" in Russia, eastern Europe, and Asia; and Barr's, at its own level, continues to dominate its domestic market.

Although the American brands did not succeed in Britain when they were first introduced around 1930, they took hold in the post-war period, having been made popular by the US armed forces. At that time the domestic market was fragmented: Barr's was among dozens of regional operators who usually served their own local market, and rarely ventured any further.

In wartime, companies like these had been effectively nationalised, becoming numbered "production units" and ordered to produce specified drinks at prices set by Government. Afterwards, new food labelling regulations were proposed which would have required that the names of soft drinks should be literally true. That would have threatened products such as Barr's American Cream Soda, which was not American and did not contain cream, for example.

The plan was not implemented in full. But the Scottish company's then chairman Robert Barr sensed that he faced a problem. His company's pre-war best selling product had been called "Iron Brew". But the same name was used by several Scottish producers, and Barr was keen to establish and retain the rights. The problem was that, strictly speaking, the sweet drink did not actually contain the required 0.125mg of iron per fluid ounce; nor was it literally "brewed".

Then Barr had a brainwave, inspired by a promotional cartoon the company had been running for several years in the Glasgow newspaper, The Bulletin. The Adventures of Ba-Bru was aimed at children, and sought to promote the drink. Barr decided to register the phonetic spelling of "Iron Brew" - "Irn-Bru" - for his product. And so a legendary brand was born.

Barr's claims that the distinctive drink has no less than 32 flavours. Its essence - the special mix of ingredients for the syrup that forms the base of all soft drinks - is reputedly known to only two members of the Barr family, and locked securely in the vaults of a Scottish bank. Whatever the secret, Irn-Bru has become a way of life for many Scots: among its many claimed attributes is its power to cure a hangover.

The company had an unusual start, and because of its growth, it retained an unusual structure prior to its Stock Market flotation in 1965. Until the late 1950s it was in fact two companies - the original based in Falkirk, its companion in Glasgow - owned by the same family, but with different share holdings. A "gentleman's agreement" existed whereby the two did not move onto each other's patch. "There was an imaginary line somewhere around Cumbernauld," laughs Robin Barr. Appropriately, he has recently centralised Scottish bottling operations in a new factory at Cumbernauld itself.

"For many years the Irn-Bru label bore the statement 'none genuine without this signature'. But the two labels carried a different signature," recalls Barr.

The company can trace its history as far back as 1830, when the first Robert Barr started a cork-cutting business in Falkirk. Cork was used for all sorts of bottles, such as for mineral drinks, beer, and medicine. But as screw-tops became available, cork was popular only with the wine market, and business faltered. Sensing a need to change tack, Barr's son, also Robert, set up as an "aerated water manufacturer" in the town in 1880, and seven years later, his son - this time Robert Fulton Barr - started a similar soft drinks' operation in Glasgow's Gallowgate. The Glasgow firm was taken over by a brother, Andrew G. Barr, who lent his name to the modern-day company.

The Falkirk company launched its "Iron Brew" in 1901, and A.G. Barr, which formally came into existence in 1904, produced the same "brew" in Glasgow. The latter company grew much more quickly, because of the city's greater population, and it eventually took over the Falkirk business formally in 1959, largely so that long-standing death duties could be paid off.

Robin Barr believes that the post-war decision to register Irn-Bru as a trade mark helped establish Barr's blend as the definitive version. He says too that, even though it is thought generally that marketing is much more competitive today, Barr's would have been described as an ambitious marketer as far back as the 1920s. "The Ba-Bru cartoons and the poster campaigns of those days were very aggressive," he points out.

His own corporate lineage is complicated. The 1904 Barr company had five founding shareholders, including A.G. Barr, R.F. Barr, and W.S. Barr, all brothers. R.F. Barr's son Robert was next in line to run the business, followed by his cousin - also Robert - who was the son of W.S. Barr. The latter Robert ran the company until 1978, when his son Robin took over operations.

Robin was the first of a generation which did not go straight into the business from school. He spent five years training as a chartered accountant before joining formally in 1960. He does remember that during the famous hot summer of 1955, when demand for soft drinks was running high, he was drafted in at the age of 17 as "relief syrup girl" in Falkirk. The usual "girl", actually a woman in her fifties, could not work the hastily-arranged additional overnight shifts, and Robin's task was to work in the syrup room as production was temporarily increased.

By 1960, having merged the two companies, the Barr's board was determined to move ahead. It competed with a broad variety of Scottish producers such as Dunn & Moore and Struthers - both still operating today - and other, now defunct, names such as Garvey and Barrie. Although it was the most successful, it wanted to expand further.

The board also had to address the demands of a growing army of shareholders, many of whom had inherited their shares in the company, but who had no direct connection with it. Its private status meant that they could not cash in their investments if they wished. And the incoming Labour Government in 1964 was planning to introduce Capital Gains Tax for the first time. Barr's decided to go public and float 25 per cent of its stock.

"There were five original shareholders, all brothers and sisters. But by 1964 there was a greatly increased number of around 30, some of whom I had never met and would never meet. They were locked into the company with no avenue to realise the investment. Apart from the tax issue, the longer term reason was to provide an automatic exit route for members of the family who were so distant that they no longer voted," explains Robin.

Barr's faced a dilemma. For tax reasons, as a private company, its shares had been valued for the benefit of the Inland Revenue at two shillings and a penny (Just over ten pence) each. Yet they floated soon afterwards at nine shillings and threepence (46p). It was becoming an increasingly common situation for family businesses, forced to float during that period either because of crippling death duties, or because remote shareholders wanted to take their money and run. Many British family companies were founded during the late 19th century and after the first world war, and their descendants were selling out to the growing number of Stock Market traded conglomerates, especially in the food and drinks sector.

Robin Barr emphasises today that strictly speaking this is no longer a family company. But the family name is an essential part of the brand in many parts of the country, and particularly Scotland. He and the other "family" shareholders account for 20 to 25 per cent of voting rights, with 10 or 15 per cent more attributable to more distant members who inherited shares and kept part of the legacy. "I can still recognise on the share register quite substantial shareholders by name. Some I know are distant third cousins whom I have never met, but who still have a very large investment in the company," he believes. "I do not want to stop that, but do I think of them as 'family'? Probably not, although there might be some influence over the way they vote."

He and his second cousin Michael are the only Barrs left on the board, his uncle Greig having stood down as a non-executive director after 46 years in 1995. But Robin Barr believes the transition from private to public company has made little difference to the company's business style since the 1960s. "Operationally there was no real change. We are a public company with a substantial family interest, but we do not really do things differently. In a strange sort of way it has not altered at all. For example, by 1967 the board consisted of three Barrs and two professional managers, and today the executive is two Barrs and three others."

More crucial to the company's astonishing growth during that period were its first cross-border raids on England's regional soft drinks' sector. Barr's had bought a Bradford firm, Hollow's, in 1955, and 10 years later it bought the larger Frucose business in Sunderland. It moved into the canned drinks' market when it bought Stotherts of Atherton in 1967. Barr's Irn-Bru was on the move.

The real breakthrough came in 1972, when Barr's bought what was effectively its English equivalent, Tizer, a top brand especially in the north of England. There Tizer had become as familiar a name as Irn-Bru was in Scotland. The history and nature of Tizer's demise as an independent operator underlined the belief within Barr's that it had indeed taken the right route to survival.

Tizer was the brainchild of a Manchester man called Fred Pickup. He and his brother dabbled in the soft drinks' business in Portsmouth and Bristol, before buying a small firm in Pudsey, Yorkshire, in 1910. Further expansion continued in Bradford, Leeds, and Manchester, and Tizer - coined from the word "appetiser" - was launched in 1924.

It was a big hit. From Manchester, Pickup controlled a virtually national company with factories as far north as Glasgow and south as Southampton and London. But Tizer moved into a long slow decline after the Second World War.

Robin Barr takes up the story: "Tizer was really the equivalent of A.G. Barr in England. It was a very successful operation with 20 locations. The company ossified because Fred Pickup would not let go. When he was 86 he still made every decision within the business until his death in the late 1960s. The whole industry had moved to non-returnable bottles, the big breakthrough in the market, but Tizer did not move into non-returnable lines, because returnable bottles were good enough for him, and they always had been."

It was indeed the advent of non-returnable containers - first cans, then plastic bottles - which allowed the soft drinks companies to "go national". Production and delivery costs were slashed. The supermarkets chains, already becoming a powerful force during the 1960s, and the absolutely dominant market players today, refused to handle returnable glass bottles. Old Mr Pickup, a classic entrepreneur of his time, witnessed his cherished company's decline because he had refused to recognise the need for change.

The company fell into the hands of a financial group on his death, and Barr's snapped it up for just £2.5m: As a guide, Barr's annual sales at the time were £5.694m to Tizer's £3.551m. One of Barr's first decisions was to research the original prewar Tizer recipe, and attempt to restore it as closely as possible to the drink whose marketing had described it as "the taste which defies description". The Tizer tale is a salutary one for British industry, and typifies the ownership dilemma faced by hundreds of family-owned companies since the war and the massive technological progress that followed.

Robin Barr believes that smaller Scottish operators, often contemporaries of the Barr operation, "faded because they were never anything more than regional, and in some cases district, suppliers". He points out: "When modern media opportunities to create branding became available, such as TV advertising, they simply could not match the marketing power of the bigger companies and they failed to make the move into new forms of packaging as they became available."

The new packaging offered soft drinks firms their biggest breakthrough. They had had to use returnable glass bottles for decades, and attempts to introduce more lightweight versions had not been successful. Today's familiar third-of-a-litre can became available in the early 1960s, to be joined later by the lighter weight aluminium versions.

But the huge opportunity arrived with plastic bottling in 1978. Apart from its immense suitability for the supermarkets, this packaging, called PET (Poly Ethylene Teraphthalite), allowed producers to deliver their drinks in anything up to three litre bottles: a huge cost advantage and also an easier way to sell more liquid for less money. The market exploded.

Barr's joined its big-time competitors in the marketing battle. The "Made in Scotland" TV advertising campaign was a direct descendant of the old "Ba-Bru" newspaper cartoon character. The Glasgow company has had to modify its sales image to accommodate English as well as Scottish tastes, but it bows to no-one in its aggressive branding. It has to do so, as its major competitors are massive world players with huge financial reserves and global TV campaigns which dwarf the powers of many other industries, with the exception of those manufacturing soap-powder, automobiles, and oil.

Barr's may be third in Britain, but in total sales' terms it is a long way behind the top two. Coca Cola/Schweppes Beverages has UK sales of £900m, and Britvic enjoys a turnover of £600m. Those figures put Barr's impressive figure of £110m in some perspective. But the company remains a strong British independent, and continues to squeeze out some more market share.

"Life was not meant to be a bed of roses. We are a good sight better placed than other companies," comments Robin Barr. "Number three was achieved by buying other businesses in England.

"If we had remained the big Scottish company the reality is we would have remained so small that we would have had no chance of competing against the large national and international organisations. Scotland is too wee a place to create a critical mass - that is a fact of life, and if you ignore it you go the way of all flesh, like all those other companies."

He praises the foresight of his father and uncle - the two Roberts who preceded him as company chairmen - in their actions across the Border. "They realised they had to address populous areas like Yorkshire, Lancashire and the North-east of England. Tizer took us right across England and into Wales as well.

"We recognised that we had outgrown Scotland and needed a national base for our operation which allows us - however hard it is - to compete nationally against big operators and have our products on the shelves of Tesco and the others."

Meanwhile the endless marketing drive continues. To raise the profile of Irn-Bru in London, Barr's laid on free bus and Tube transport in the capital for New Year's Eve. When a Glasgow skier was rescued after spending three nights stranded on the bleak slopes above Glenshee, his first reported words to his helpers were to ask for a drink of Irn-Bru. Prompted by the resulting publicity, Barr's donated £1,000 to the mountain rescue team. No opportunity is spurned in the relentless drive both to build market share in Britain and protect Irn-Bru's number one position in Scotland.

The key market for all soft-drinks' manufacturers is for consumers aged 16 to 24. One poster campaign shows an elderly rather professorial-looking doctor advising: "Irn-Bru can't make you pregnant. But it can make you a bit frisky."

Meanwhile the new bottling plant in Cumbernauld, 108,000 square feet set in 22 acres with room for expansion, includes two lines which can package drinks at the rate of up to 30,000 bottles per hour. A far cry from those early days in Falkirk where bottles were packed carefully into boxes by hand, and the most modern innovation was a conveyor belt. Modern graphics are added to the marketing mix. Dandelion & Burdock, a popular brand in the north of England, has been "repackaged" there as "D&B", in an attempt to attract younger consumers.

Irn-Bru is being exported too, across Europe and into Russia. It is advertised on TV in Bahrain. And there are regular marketing campaigns in South Africa and Canada. The once-humble Scottish soft drink is itching to become a truly international brand.

It is a beguiling drink, very sweet and a vivid reddish-orange in colour. Scots drink it by the gallon, intrigued by those 32 flavours which turn into one. It may or may not cure a hangover. It can only be Irn-Bru. Yet it does not really contain iron, and it has never been brewed. But as the advertisement says: "It's Made in Scotland. So You Canny Complain!"

CHAPTER EIGHT

Two generations on the road

John Russell, the unassuming boss of Scotland's biggest independent haulage firm, has always been a bit of a trouble-shooter. One of his early tests during the 1960s came at Smithfield Market in London, where porters had "blacked" two trucks loaded with Scotch lamb, because their trailers were eight feet longer than the norm.

Russell had introduced the new 32-foot trailers, in order to increase their carrying capacity for what was in those days a long-haul journey. This was the early 1960s, during the era in British industry when management and unions were entrenched in mutual opposition, a situation highlighted at the time by the celebrated Peter Sellars' comedy film, I'm Alright Jack.

The new trailer lengths meant that the porters would have to carry the lamb carcasses a further eight feet. Despite a day spent making several desperate telephone calls, Russell - then the 26 year old boss of his own small Scottish haulage business - was told that his trucks would stand overnight, still unloaded. He arranged immediately to meet the Smithfield shop steward and took the sleeper south for the 7am rendezvous.

"It was freezing cold at Smithfield, and seemed even colder surrounded by carcasses, and the steward suggested we have a hot drink. An excellent idea," recalls Russell. After three hours of talks, and more refreshments, a deal was reached which was to form the basis of a long-standing relationship for the company at the market. The "hot drink" turned out to have been warmed rum and peppermint. "I have never resorted to the same breakfast again," laughs Russell.

On another occasion Russell had a problem with dockers at Southampton, offended by a driver who had taken out his frustration about a delay. Another lengthy meeting ensued, followed by dinner, during which the local union representative refused to join the meal. Nevertheless, the relationship warmed, and soon the same man had a change of heart and was showing Russell and his colleagues around his native city with great enthusiasm.

The days of lorries being "blacked" on such apparently minor technicalities are long gone from the haulage trade. Delivery times are everything these days, and technology, along with better equipment and more reliable transport have combined to take haulage into the cutting edge of manufacturing industry. But the anecdotes are important to John Russell in explaining his philosophy that personal relationships are crucial in his business. In more modern times that has remained key to his progress at the head of a group which includes six operating subsidiaries, employs 420 people, keeps more than 200 vehicles on the road, and turns over around £20m a year.

Russell's father and grandfather had been in the transport business, and John himself served his time with his father's haulage business in West Lothian. But at 17, in 1954, he had thought first of a career in farming. Soon afterwards he waited in his lawyer's office after putting in a bid for a small holding in Edinburgh, only to find he had lost out. Discouraged, he turned back to the family business.

The eldest of seven children, he clearly felt he had something to prove. At 20 he set up on his own account, launching a series of adventures, including the minor crisis in Smithfield, before selling out to the national Transport Development Group (TDG), in 1964. "They never visited the business, they just paid on the basis of the accounts," he remembers. John moved to work for the company in London, but his experience there was to prompt him to set out on his own all over again.

"I found working in a large group doubly onerous: first of all you had to work out in your own mind what you should do. But after that you had to convince your board that it should be done. That can be a good thing, but decisions were long-winded and often taken that were impartial to the situation," believes John.

He was used as a troubleshooter by TDG, first to settle a dispute at Barking, and then another in Airdrie. He returned to Scotland to manage five TDG-owned businesses, but became disillusioned quickly by internal politics. One day in 1968 he discovered that a less senior manager had been promoted to the board without his knowledge. "It seems petty now, but it really brought home the point that this was not for me," he recalls. Having just signed a new five year contract, he resigned, "giving four years and nine months' notice," he laughs. He escaped sooner than that: for Russell, now 32 and father of four young children, it was time to become self-employed once more in 1969.

He bought an Airdrie haulage business, John Alexander & Sons, which had gone bust, but had 12 vehicles and a reasonable customer base. Russell's former contract required him to agree that he would not compete directly with TDG-owned companies in Scotland for a minimum five years. But he soon spotted an opportunity at nearby Gartcosh, and won work from the then British Steel Corporation for its finishing-mill there. Russell renamed his business John G. Russell Transport, and moved the short distance to Gartcosh.

The Russell operation of today is unrecognisable from the rough and ready business of the early 1970s. For John Russell has continued to use his keen sense of timing within the industry to spot trends and react to them in order to survive and remain profitable.

During the 1970s he bought Carntyne Transport in Glasgow, which had a steady business in delivering whisky casks for the old Distillers Company. The business was owned by his father's own firm, which had planned to close it down, but John bought it out instead. That was followed by another takeover target, R.D. Spittal. His next important acquisition was of Deanside Transit at Hillington, to the west of Glasgow, in 1983.

The key change in the haulage business during that period had been the switch to using containers, which slashed costs for operators. But that heralded an increasingly competitive market: the average price of delivering a 20 ton load from Glasgow to London was cut so far as to be virtually unprofitable. Russell realised that to survive he had to broaden his business base, and get into warehousing as well as haulage.

Today, Russell works in a high-tech, lean cost system, taking on more and more non-haulage work for customers. Manufacturers and importers will hand over a load, and leave the time consuming task of disaggregating its contents and repackaging them for local delivery to Russell. Its warehouses are streamlined, with every item bar-coded so that each driver knows which loads are to go where.

Most manufacturers, whether in food or electronics, now operate the "just in time" system, whereby components and parts are supplied only at the time when they are needed. Finished products are given far more exact delivery schedules. Adapting to those demands requires a haulage company to be much more than a simple means of transferring product "from A to B and back again".

Russell now holds 1.5 million square feet of warehousing, several depots around the UK - most with rail connections - as well as operating one of Britain's biggest container transport systems. It will shrink-wrap product on behalf of customers, and its fleet includes special tankers for carrying anything from sugars and glucose to molasses and beer.

At Carntyne, drivers no longer tour the Highland distilleries simply to load casks of malt. They drive bulk tankers, and Russell takes a hand in packaging a huge share of Scotland's annual whisky output for export. By adding work the company has added value to its service, and profited from it. It is a tribute to an essentially "regional" company based in Scotland that it has continued to hold contracts with Distillers' successor company, United Distillers, since its takeover by Guinness. Russell can compete comfortably with the national hauliers on long-distance or "primary" transport. But the company does not have a UK-wide local distribution network.

It has spent many years developing its railway links, specialising in so-called "inter modal" transport, whereby loads can be interchanged between road and rail trucks. All of this activity resulted from John Russell's ability to adapt quickly to changing market demands. He believes that fact more than compensates for his not being a "big" national operator.

A few years ago the wiseacres of the haulage trade were predicting the demise of the small and medium sized operators, or companies like Russell, with its strong base in a comparatively small part of the market, Scotland. "I recall being told by one man 'You're going to have to sell out. Everything will be controlled by the big boys'. But in fact we have made our mark, and we have often satisfied customers far better than those big fellows," believes Russell.

He admits that he was worried then, when it seemed that many manufacturers, having rationalised their own transport operations, were likely to hand over their entire haulage business to UK national operators. "It was a threat. We can do Scotland, from primary transport to High Street delivery, but not the local stuff in England. But progressively by monitoring our own quality of service, we have developed our reputation, and things have worked out." adds Russell.

Today all four Russell children work full time for the company's various divisions, and John's wife Isobel remains on the main board. Graham, who joined as an apprentice welder at 17, runs the Gartcosh business, while Kenneth is in a senior position at Deanside. Daughters Elizabeth Ann, in charge of packaging at Deanside, and Shireen, working in the Storage Services subsidiary in Leith, complete the family circle.

Shares are spread across the family, and Russell is determined that the company remain independent. "I think it gives us a big advantage. We are only vulnerable if we do not perform, but we are not vulnerable to the vagaries of the Stock Market, where someone might put in a bid. We have to make sure that we progress in a way that protects all 420 of us in the company," believes John.

71

He has not accorded special treatment to his children, although they are taking on ownership through equity transfers, and will undoubtedly have a major role in future. So far only Graham, aged 31, has actually joined his parents on the main board, which includes several trusted executives such as company secretary Morag Wigfield, finance director Kenneth Macleod, and Alec Pearson, who has special responsibilities for training and quality control across the business. Other senior managers include Brian Harkness, who runs Carntyne Transport, and Graham Winton, recruited recently from the food group Asda to be managing director at Deanside.

John has no intention of retiring soon, adding that there are too many exciting developments to look forward to in the transport and haulage sector. He says that there is no fixed management succession plan, and does not rule out a non-family member replacing him eventually. But he adds that his children all work hard, and that he could see one or more of them developing as a direct successor. The nature of the group's structure means that each of the children has been able to develop their abilities and experience without "living in each other's pockets", as Graham puts it.

His father has become a respected figure in the industry, becoming the first and only "regional" member of the national Freight Transport Association, and an important player within the Confederation of British Industry in Scotland. He keeps a keen eye on transport and infrastructural issues, from the controversial "road pricing" plans to hand over new road development to the private sector to the transition to rail transport for long-haul and Continental haulage.

Russell can claim with some justification to some far-sighted decisions in the past, having become involved in rail freight for many years, lobbying for greater access to the rail network, long before privatisation was mooted. The Deanside operation has a substantial railhead system for transporting whisky and other goods, long before rail privatisation was first mooted. He believes that, regardless of politics, concern about traffic congestion and other environmental issues will lead to increased pressure to invest in rail freight from both UK and European governmental levels. That trend is one of the "exciting" developments ahead which deter him from making any plans for retirement.

He puts great emphasis on fostering an "informal" management structure which encourages employees to speak their mind and participate in the company's development, his only requirement being that "everyone remains focused on serving the customer". He points out that there is a low staff turnover - unusual in the haulage sector - and has recently extended the company pension scheme and introduced a profit-sharing system. "We do not pay ourselves dividends, just salaries. Everything is reinvested in the company," adds Russell.

The boss himself has been known to remove his jacket, roll up his shirt-sleeves and help out in the warehouse if there is a deadline problem with a delivery. Recently he spent 48 hours doing just that during a "minor crisis". Russell believes the family's individual roles within the company are vital to developing internal relationships. "We have far more flexibility, but our key strength is that we are all pretty close to the ground. If something is not quite right we can influence it more quickly. We are extremely sensitive to the customer's needs," believes Russell.

One weakness in remaining independent is that the Russell group's access to funds is limited when compared to those of its national competitors, but Russell believes "that just means we have to tailor our opportunities".

He admits that he has been criticised - "by my wife usually" - for not making more of a direct effort to train and encourage his children, perhaps grooming them more overtly to take over. When they were young, John says he did not think it right to push them into the business, believing: "They had to make up their own minds." But he adds that he was very pleased when each of his children did join.

Kenneth arrived shortly after his younger brother Graham, having tried university life first. He worked as a driver, before running a small company depot in Inverness. Recently he has agreed to concentrate on marketing at Deanside, the need to have somebody working full time on developing new business being a reflection of the increasingly competitive nature of the industry.

John admits he could have been more forceful in guiding the children directly into the business. "But I have tried by giving them opportunities that they can cope with. I had no education beyond O Grade. I learned by experience and I cannot say I have regretted that, in fact there is a lot of merit in it," explains Russell. "I do not expect things to be done my way only. Very often there are different ways of doing something. So if someone reaches the required standard in a cost-effective way, that is fine."

Certainly the approach seems to have worked. Like the others, Graham started within the company at the bottom, first as a welding apprentice, and then serving his time as a mechanic. He spent a year in the Gartcosh office before heading off to Australia during his twenties to work for two distribution companies in Melbourne, quickly becoming traffic manager for one firm at the city's docks, and then moving into an office job. "I wanted to see how other companies operated and broaden my outlook of the industry generally. I have worked with a lot of people in the company back here over the years, so I know them as colleagues," points out Graham. He adds that he has "no apprehensions" about moving up the management ladder in the family firm as a result.

"This is a service industry and in transport all sorts of things can go wrong, so the challenge is to operate with the customer in mind. You follow things through: you hopefully develop the customer's business along with them."

Graham remembers working for his father during school holidays - "changing the odd wheel as a kid" - and is clearly keen to play a role in the future of the business, explaining: "We are trying to look at how the company is going to progress over 10, 20 or 30 years."

The very fact that a company should be looking so far ahead indicates one clear strength of remaining independent. One of the long-stated criticisms of the Stock Market is that analysts push listed companies into thinking only of the short-term. Strategy may be important, but it often takes second place to keep shareholders and their brokers satisfied with regular dividends. That is anathema to an owner-manager like John Russell, who places such great faith in personal business relationships.

One key factor in the company's success with the whisky and food manufacturers has been its willingness to fit in with their changing requirements and styles of operation. Russell spotted that many big operators were moving to concentrate on their core business, and were increasingly prepared as a result to farm out peripheral work such as haulage, warehousing and packaging. The new partnerships wrought from that change helped the business through its stickiest periods.

Russell's greatest crisis came in 1991, when an international customer signed a deal which involved Russell committing his company to building a state-of-the-art £1.7m warehouse at Hillington. Work had no sooner begun than the client changed its mind. The only communication Russell received was a faxed letter cancelling the deal, at the end of the same week as contracts had been exchanged and work begun. "We were caught both ways, because the building we sold in Glasgow to fund the new building went to Rush & Tompkins just as they were liquidated."

The memory is a harsh one for Russell personally. His conversation is peppered with references to integrity in business. He points out that most of his deals with major customers such as Distillers have often been settled "on a handshake". The 1991 experience was clearly hurtful - Russell admits "it took us a long time to get over it" - and could have undermined the company, had it not been for a long and trusting relationship with its bank. The company's profits started to grow again only three years later.

John Russell remains a big fish in the Scottish pool within the haulage business. He is clearly proud to have continued a tradition involving both his father and grandfather, and it was important for him to set up on his own account, something he had had to do all over again after selling out to one of the "big boys" of the British market.

He sees the future as a question of maintaining the position in Scotland, building at a British level, and becoming more attuned to European transport needs. And he attaches great importance to maintaining contact with everyone involved in his business: increasingly that will involve helping his children develop their own roles within it.

"My heart has always been in transport. We have been courted by three international companies over the years, but I hope we will never be required to sell our souls," reflects Russell. "And looking back, I am glad that farm was sold to someone else!"

CHAPTER NINE

A Family Business Adapting to Change

In a stark office suite overlooking Glasgow's George Square - itself the scene of many tumultuous moments in the city's turbulent history - the fifth generation of one of Scotland's most familiar High Street names is grappling with the forces of change.

Malcolm Campbell's stores, created by a former message boy who took over his boss's business in 1878, is synonymous with the independent grocery trade. Generations have bought their fruit and vegetables in one or other of its branches, which once numbered 70 throughout Scotland.

The company proudly introduced the tomato and the banana to Scottish society. Its history, its successes and failures, has parallels with the rise and fall of Glasgow and Scotland's standing in the modern world, as well as its virtual rebirth. Social trends can be detected simply by reading the history of this very essentially Scottish company.

It was founded by Malcolm Campbell, who had arrived in Glasgow aged 15 with six years' work experience behind him (at nine he had become head of the family after the premature death of his coal miner father in a pit accident), to work as a messenger for a city fruiterer, Mark Walker. His wage was six shillings a week, and he worked on for 14 years until his employer decided to emigrate to Canada and sold him the business.

Campbell opened his first store in 1878, and prospered. Servants flooded his stores with their daily orders; "ladies of the house" would alight from their carriages in Gordon Street to peruse the stalls, it being fashionable for them to make their own selections of fruit and vegetables. Glasgow was the second city of the British Empire: bustling and prosperous, and a major trading city.

Campbell imported grapes, peaches, celery and spring onions from the south of France; green grapes and melons from Almeria and oranges from Seville; apples from everywhere, and new potatoes from the Channel Islands. He introduced the banana - a great delicacy at the time - and the tomato to the Glasgow palate, for whom "fruit" had been a simple and mundane diet of apples and pears. In one day in 1911, three and a half tons of strawberries were delivered to the main store at the corner of Gordon Street and West Nile Street: a record at the time.

The poor Ayrshire miner's son became a merchant grandee, and a local Justice of the Peace. Just as with the tea merchant Matthew Algie, whose fortunes are recorded elsewhere in this book, hard work brought prosperity, and wealth brought influence. Campbell was a popular and well-known business man, and something of a dandy. A contemporary account noted: "In summer he came on the job each day wearing a light grey morning suit with starched stock and top hat to match; fresh flower in his lapel and spotless spats above the smartest hand-made shoes Scottish craftsmanship could provide. He had one suede glove on his left hand in which the other glove was carried, the right hand being occupied by an elegant walking cane, which its owner swung sedately on occasions. He was tall, well-made and possessed what is known as 'presence'."

A far cry from descriptions of the businessmen of today, littered as they are with accounts of the latest merger or acquisition, and obsessed with stock dividends and leverage. In Victorian and Edwardian times, businessmen were "gentlemen", devoted to the Scottish ethic of hard work and thrift. They were pre-eminent, and many of them also made considerable personal fortunes.

At the great Glasgow International Exhibition of 1901, in Kelvingrove, Campbell's had its own pavilion, replete with company flag. The company, sharing the confidence of its home city, faced the world in the knowledge that it was an important economic and trading presence. No-one had dreamt up Asda or Tesco, and not even the Americans had thought of a supermarket: new developments which were to undermine the success of thousands of businesses like Campbell's in the latter half of the 20th century.

Campbell himself was shrewd and innovative. Apart from introducing the banana - a virtually unheard of luxury - during the 1890s, he became wholesaler to his competitors as well as building his retail chain. He opened his first fruit and confectionery kiosk in Glasgow's St. Enoch railway station in 1904, and soon developed a chain of 60, stretching from Stonehaven to

Crewe. He had 200 staff, and had begun to introduce motor transport to augment his fleet of horse-led carts by the outbreak of war in 1914.

The founder lived until 1935, when he was 87. Sadly his son Dr. Malcolm Campbell and grandson Malcolm Brown Campbell both died a lot younger, in 1937 and 1940. The company passed to the younger Malcolm's widow, Helen, who - assisted by Glasgow accountant Robert Browning, who became chairman - ran the business until her son, another Malcolm and great grandson of the founder, took over in 1968. Helen continued to play an active role in the company for nearly 20 years, as a board director.

Glasgow in the 1960s was no longer an industrial and economic powerhouse. It could not be second city of the Empire, as the Empire had disappeared. Campbell's, with 70 stores between Aberdeen and Carlisle and a fair number of railway station kiosks surviving, was a significant company, but in a shrinking market.

The reason was simple. The mini-markets and grocery stores were becoming larger and beginning to merge ownership, and the fledgling chains which were to become the supermarket giants like Safeway and Tesco were beginning to make their presences felt in the High Streets across Britain. Malcolm himself had trained with Cooper's Finefare, a family-owned chain which was to be swallowed up by the major players in the years to come.

Trends had changed too. Between the 1960s and 1980s, popular stores in the city centre were no longer so busy. Office workers bought their food supplies either in supermarkets at the weekend or in local corner shops at night. Campbell responded by stepping up its distribution activities, and by augmenting the number of goods on its shelves, including tinned foods, meat and cheese. A central office and warehouse was established in Rutherglen. Campbell's was among hundreds of family businesses being forced to adapt to the harsh realities of the modern marketplace.

The fourth-generation Malcolm adapted well. He had to make tough decisions about the spread of activities. City stores were performing less well. The warehousing facility was becoming burdensome, simply because many suppliers began to deliver directly to stores rather than to a central point for distribution later. Campbell knew he could not take on the superstores, and reasoned that he might well join them: the company became a buyer for the Asda chain. Meanwhile its string of stores fell from 70 to 40 or 50, and down to 23.

That in turn created the need to rebalance the company's activities, a large part of which had become not food retailing, but property management. Campbell's owned most of its sites, rather than leasing them, and now makes a considerable proportion of its income from managing that portfolio. The rethinking has allowed for improved direction of priorities for the shops, whose number has risen again to 27.

Crucially it became time for another hand over of management to the next generation. Malcolm, aged 62, has two sons in the business now. Managing director David, aged 33, joined the company after gaining experience with Asda and a South African chain, Pick'n'Pay. He has been joined by Graham, who worked previously as a produce manager for the Darlington based North of England supermarket chain Morrison's, and then in public relations with the large London-based consultancy Shandwick.

Theirs has been a text-book case of what is called "succession management", the transfer of ownership and direction from one generation to another. The theory of succession may seem simple, but in practice it is fraught with pitfalls, and has caused many companies to sell out or go bust as a result of irredeemable personality clashes, ignorance, or plain bad luck.

Stewart Clark, Glasgow based partner for the accountancy firm BDO Stoy Hayward and a specialist in the family business sector, says that often the problem of succession comes down to personalities. "It is not unusual for the chairman or founder of a business to be a very dominant personality. He keeps all the important matters in his head, and does not communicate details to his sons or daughters, even when they work in the company. When the time comes for succession, it can be chaos."

Clark has witnessed situations where brothers have come to blows about the running of the company, or where the father has handed over to someone other than the eldest child amid deep family bitterness and division. "I once had to counsel someone for four or five hours because he had come to the point of breakdown because of tension with his brother about the direction of the company. He just poured everything out," remembers Clark."The basic problem is that many company founders think they are immortal. The succession is never brought up in conversation. Sometimes where there is more than one child working in the business they have not even discussed it between themselves," reflects Clark.

The Campbells took the sensible route. Malcolm prepared a buy-out for peripheral shareholders: people, often distant relatives, who had inherited shares over the years but played no role in the running of the company. That consolidation means that the company is owned 100 per cent by Malcolm and his sister Lorna, and David and Graham as well as their elder brother Colin, aged 35, who is not involved in the company, having pursued his own career in the food retailing sector.

Malcolm chairs the board, which includes David and Graham as well as two non-family directors, Fiona Milloy, a property specialist who rose through the management ranks, and long-serving senior manager Tom Leighton, who plays a key role with David in fruit market dealings and the day to day running of the retail business. The chairman is reducing his presence in the company and spending less time in the George Square office as his management team, including two of his sons, takes over.

"There has never been any pressure to join the company, but I always had it at the back of my mind, and I know David had always wanted to be here from very early on," says Graham, aged 29, who joined the family company in 1991 as a management trainee. "I genuinely believe that we had to have something to offer the business in terms of experience.

"Dad spent a lot of time working on the buy-back. It is very complicated because somebody has to work out just what shares in a family company are worth, and there are tax implications too. It took about two years to complete.

"I think we have all been very realistic about the transition between one generation and another. We are relatively rare in being a fifth generation family business," believes David. "We have done positive things, such as quite deliberately keeping two non-family members on the board to balance things. We have always listened to advice and taken it too. There are times within a family company when you need somebody outside the family to offer a 'reality check'."

The process of change has stretched back for nearly 20 years, largely because of the superstores' phenomenon. Campbell's has had to adapt to growing public demand for convenience and variety. The number of lines available in its stores has leapt from 300 to 3,000 over the years. Instead of city shops, many of the retail sites are in urban areas, open "eight till late", to allow people to pick up extras in the evening after work, or before they leave for work in the morning. The range goes far beyond traditional fruit and vegetable fare, to include delicatessen goods such as salami and imported cheeses, and even ice cream.

"Our presence has to be as a neighbourhood store. We need places which will be busy all the time, rather than only during certain periods of the day," explains Graham. Another recent innovation has been Campbell's development of in-store concessions within the growing Kwiksave chain, whereby the Glasgow firm supplies and runs the fruit and vegetable area of some of the chain's stores under the larger firm's name.

Campbell's is run in a highly disciplined fashion. Its sales administration is based at the Glasgow Fruit Market. Fruit is one of the most perishable products, and buying decisions are crucial in order to minimise ways and maximise turnover. The company's 27 store managers - all women - place their orders with the company's tele-sales department at the market daily, and deliveries are made either from the company's market base, or direct from suppliers. The actual trading decisions are made by David Campbell and long-serving director Tom Leighton.

"We have changed over the years to having management from the bottom up. The managers meet once a month and go through stock, waste, wages and so on," says Graham.

"We have had to change with the times. Our Rutherglen office was designed in the 1960s to supply more than 50 stores, but the number had fallen. Now all the meat, cheese, milk and bread will be delivered direct by suppliers anyway, so our main buying and distribution is concentrated at the market.

"The death of family companies especially in the food retailing business has been down to their inability to change. There are not many left, and the problem was they were too frightened to change. It is very hard to do, especially when it involves rationalisation. But you have to keep looking for new ways of increasing your turnover to survive."

The company moved to its tiny head office in George Square in 1989, reflecting the need for low cost management and greater efficiency. It began to embrace the competition rather than succumbing to it, initially by taking a contract to buy and pack produce for the growing Asda chain.

Malcolm senior, like his great grandfather a stickler for quality, once bought an entire stock of Brussels sprouts from his Dundee store, rather than have them examined by a supermarket inspector, and brought them home in the boot of his car simply because they did not appear to reach the necessary standard.

A family business is an intimate affair. It is not unusual for a manager to be asked by one of his branches which type of strip-light should be purchased for the store. If that manager happens to be a family member, then he or she has to know such apparently trivial detail in order to prove to the staff that they are committed to the business. That is one reason why so many children enter the business at a comparatively low level, such as management trainee, in order to learn the business at every level.

"When I joined the business they did not know what I was capable of and also when you are working with your brother it is essential to establish your working relationship. The natural thing for me to do was to help run one side of the business while David runs another side. There is a clear definition of roles," points out Graham.

David took over as managing director in 1994, concentrating on the retail and buying areas. Their father made a clear decision to pass on to the next generation when he was 60, and is scaling down his involvement. The family relied heavily on its trusted advisers, including lawyers and accountants, to help manage the process of change itself, including the shares' buyback.

There is a clear determination within Campbell's to remain independent. Its survival as a fifth generation is the result of careful planning and a willingness to change in one of the most dynamic retail sectors. The original Malcolm, the man who dragged himself up from nothing to enjoy Victorian prosperity chiefly by innovating within his own market-place, would likely approve.

CHAPTER TEN

Phoenix from the Flames

At 2am one Friday morning in June 1995, Shazia Gallam had been finding it difficult to sleep. She and her husband Wazir and three sons were in their Edinburgh home when the telephone rang. It was a call which would literally change the couple's lives and test their characters to the limits.

On the other end of the line was the manager of Abel Eastern's manufacturing plant 15 miles away in Livingston. There was a fire, he said, come quickly. "I do not understand to this day why I had not fallen asleep that night. When the call came I didn't even ask how bad the fire was or anything. We just went there immediately," recalls Shazia.

When the owners arrived at Livingston's Houstoun industrial estate, they stood in shock and watched as vicious flames leapt through the roof of their cherished factory building. Firefighters used thousands of gallons of water before managing to control the blaze: too late, as the factory had been gutted.

After a decade of scrimping and sacrifice which had helped grow a unique business whose national sales were approaching £10m, Wazir and Shazia saw their dream go up literally in smoke. "I just stood there looking at the fire and thought 'well this is the end of my life'," confesses Shazia. "I really thought that nothing more could be done."

Abel and its few British competitors use highly specialised gas ovens in the manufacturing of nan bread and other so-called "ethnic foods". The powerful machines are needed to ensure high temperatures for better quality baking. On that fateful early morning of June 30th, one such oven had ignited a fire which spread so quickly and furiously through the building that little could be done to curtail it. As firefighters dowsed the flames at one end of the building, fire shot across the cavity between the ceiling and roof, and exploded through the opposite wall. Miraculously, none of the night-shift workers had been hurt, as the fire took hold during a tea break.

There was worse to come: in a bizarre twist of fate, Abel's insurers said that insurance cover had expired at midnight on the 29th, just two hours before calamity struck. The Gallams believe it was due to expire 24 hours later, and the resulting refusal to pay out is the subject of legal action at the time of writing.

No building, no production, no insurance, and no means to start up operations immediately. It seemed like the end of the world, and it had been delivered in devastating circumstances. The couple, whose business began at Shazia's kitchen table, where she had experimented in trying to cook better-quality nan breads than she had picked up from the retail stores, were back - literally - to square one.

There was an added hurt, one which cut deeply and still brings on a pained expression when it is recalled. "We had 280 staff, and we had to call them together and tell them their jobs were gone. They were upset, it was a natural reaction, but they held us responsible. People were pointing the finger, and we had some bad publicity. I understand that it was natural, they were losing their livelihoods, but we needed to be exonerated," says Shazia.

The implied accusation that somehow the fire had been deliberate, or that Wazir and Shazia had been involved, was blatantly false, and clearly untrue: no evidence was found of wilful fire-raising, and the authorities had no suspicions at all. The shock of the very accusation was painful, and remains so to this day. But in the hours and days ahead, the couple were inundated with calls and offers of help. One food manufacturer even offered Abel space in his factory to continue operations: that proved impractical; the Gallams knew that one way or another they would have to start up all over again.

"One of the banks asked what we wanted to do. I asked if they would give us £500,000 to start up in a small way and they said yes. They were not even our bank. We knew then, because so many people wanted to help, that we could start again, so we set about planning things as quickly as we could."

One major customer, Sainsbury, even put a sign on their bread shelves apologising to customers for the lack of Abel products, explaining there had been a fire at the suppliers. That was a big morale booster: Wazir and Shazia had fought hard to win orders from the supermarket chains, and here was a concrete signal of loyalty from one of the biggest names. By now, restarting Abel would simply be a matter of time.

"Pride had a lot to do with it," underlines Wazir. "There was a determination to succeed again. We crammed 12 years of experience into one year, which is difficult. We did not have time to learn to crawl and walk again, and we had a new team, but we couldn't teach them what we knew too slowly."

Within weeks, the Gallams had the bones of a funding package together. It has not been easy for this proud and independent couple to accept a loss of control, since their new investors - including Scottish Enterprise, the venture capital fund 3i, and Brown Shipley - required shareholdings in exchange for their money. But nevertheless the package was put in place by autumn of 1995, and a new production site located in Cumbernauld. "It was still a building site when we attended a big exhibition in Germany with hand-made product. We took the chance that everything would be ready quickly," says Wazir.

Within a year of the fire, in June 1996, the new company Abel Eastern International was employing 160 people at Cumbernauld, and predicting first-year sales of more than £8m: close to the level reached before the calamity in Livingston. Work was underway on an extension to the manufacturing centre, to allow for a new production line including filled bread products such as mince, spinach, and vegetable nan breads. For the first time in a year, the talk in the Cumbernauld office suite is of sales targets and production schedules, and not dominated by the dreaded memories of "the fire".

Ironically, Abel's stiffest competitor, which had cashed in during the period when the Scottish company's products were off the shelves, suffered a similar fire involving a gas oven at its premises in County Durham. Meanwhile, Abel's biggest customers were beginning to stock their products once again.

The Gallams are an intensely close and supportive couple. Both from northern England originally, they met and married in Edinburgh, before moving to the north of Scotland to follow Wazir's work as a salesman. Having married in 1979, when both were 21, they adopted traditional roles at first: Wazir was the main breadwinner, working as a salesman for a double-glazing company, before moving on to security video equipment. Shazia ran a newsagents' business near their home in Elgin, Morayshire, for a while too.

By 1983, Wazir had become deeply frustrated with his lot: disillusioned with his various jobs, and although he was determined to become self-employed, bereft of ideas about what he might do. He enjoyed the life of a salesman, and meeting people. He had made many contacts, but did not know whether or how that might be advantageous. The shop tided things over, but did not provide enough of a challenge.

"He was very restless. One day, just out of the blue, I pointed to some nan breads in a shop and told him I could make better than that. He replied 'if you can cook it I can sell it', and really the whole beginning was as silly as that," says Shazia.

"We brought some of the stuff home from a store in Aberdeen and it was absolutely dreadful. I could not understand why companies could make such rubbish and I did not believe that consumers should get such a poor quality product. That was our starting point: we wanted to sell quality products to the supermarkets."

The couple's bank matched their £3,000 savings from the shop business, and they were awarded a small business loan by the then Scottish Development Agency. Livingston Development Corporation found them a small industrial unit in the Howden area of the West Lothian new town. Shazia had been cooking nan breads at her Elgin home for many months, testing them out on family, neighbours, and friends, and checking their reactions before changing her methods. When the couple had moved south and started formal production, an early order came from the Aberdeen depot of a national firm, Deep Freeze Supplies, and soon another was won from the Scottish-owned Farmfoods chain.

From those early days Shazia was the driving force behind the company, and Wazir an affable leader, whose natural friendliness probably helped persuade potential clients to risk trying out the new products despite the company's raw start. But the couple had struck at a market sector which was developing quickly, in reflection of changing and increasingly sophisticated tastes and growing public demand for better quality.

"The problem was that the product on the market then really did not do Indian food justice. I did not believe any Indian would have eaten it, and I felt the product was far too Anglicised, just as the food in Indian restaurants used to be Anglicised. Nothing was authentic," says Shazia.

"Ethnic foods", for want of a better description, had crept on to the shelves of supermarkets and grocery stores as a follow-on to the growing success of Britain's Asian restaurants. For many years people ate curries or other exotic dishes from India, Pakistan, Bangladesh, and so on, only in restaurants, or as the habitual "carry out".

At first the menus were usually basic. But by the early 1980s restaurateurs were experimenting with new styles of food preparation. Menus became longer and more varied: sauces and mixes more exotic. The Scots have a keen taste for Asian food, and were among the vanguard in demanding more choice and better quality. Specialist restaurants were sprouting up even in Scotland's small towns. The "ethnic" food sector has been among the fastest growing for many years.

And part of the joy of eating Indian or Pakistani food is in sampling its accompaniments, whether it is yoghurt sauces or spicy onions, chapatis or tikka pieces. Pakora was augmented with all kinds of fillings and rival "starters" like samosa or dosa pancakes. Above all there was the bread:

chapati, paratha, and the ubiquitous nan: usually oval shaped, it was a giant teardrop of buttery hot bread, used to soak up the sauces and add substance to any dish.

The problem was that the best food was to be had in restaurants, and from them alone. Several attempts to transfer the same culinary experience to the supermarket deep freeze had not been successful. There were several reasons, but the primary ones were that often the manufacturers who supplied those products were not themselves specialists, having simply added the breads to their product ranges. Secondly, and crucially, making bread which is to be reheated at home is rather different from whipping it together expertly in a kitchen and producing it from the grill alongside a dish of rogan josh at the restaurant table.

This was the crucial point that Shazia grasped when she grumbled about the poor quality of the product which she had purchased in an Aberdeen store. She experimented time and again until she achieved the right balance of ingredients to produce a tasty and authentic nan bread which could be taken home, and even frozen, yet still faithfully reproduce the quality of a top Asian restaurant.

In conversation, Shazia emerges slowly as a driving force, a formidable woman whose sheer determination to succeed is masked in a quiet politeness and a delicate air. She pushed Wazir onwards when he felt down, she came up with the ideas, and she has been at the centre of every major decision which the couple have had to make since starting up in business together back in 1984. All the way along she has been forced to acquire additional skills in book-keeping, business administration, and new product development. Where he is light-hearted and affable, she is serious and analytical. They make a first-class foil.

There was a subtle change in the formation of the new Abel operation in 1995: Shazia became managing director, allowing Wazir to concentrate on his best skill in marketing. They share three sons, and a business so successful that it recovered from catastrophe with the willing and speedy help of several hard-nosed investors. And while Shazia is the driver, it was her husband who consoled her during that dark dawn in 1995 when she thought her life in business was over, once and for all. The Gallams may not stop to assess their worth too often, since both are given to 12-hour working days and a lifestyle where business and family come above all else, but they are indeed a pair of winners.

Asked if they would have succeeded in business had they not met, they agree that each has brought the best out in the other. "It needed the catalyst of both of us. In the early years it was easier as we set the pace ourselves. We had no-one to answer to, and now because of changing circumstances we have to become more structured and look at other people's ideas," responds Wazir.

"The job has changed. It is more a job of managing people now. I did finance until we became bigger, and then I hired an accountant. I looked after personnel, but now we have someone else to do that. It was happening in the old company, and it is more of an enforced discipline. But that is no bad thing," agrees Shazia.

They met in Edinburgh, although both are from Yorkshire originally. Wazir had flitted to help his brother run a newsagents' store in the Scottish capital, and studied at the local Stevenson College before doing chemistry at the University of Lancaster, a course he did not finish. Instead he returned to Scotland, got a salesman's job with Everest, and married Shazia, whose family had moved north from Huddersfield to take over a shop.

Less than five years into their marriage, their first year of trading as Abel - the name was chosen because it was simple for customers to remember and had mildly "Eastern" connotations - was hard. The couple, just 26 and with two sons already, achieved sales of £28,000, but losses were equivalent to or even slightly more than that amount. "After that first year I almost gave up," says Wazir. "But Shazia kept kicking me out of bed in the mornings and saying 'no, we will not give up this business and have you go back to selling for somebody else'. The first significant breakthrough came when Waitrose in England, which was part of the John Lewis Partnership, took our bread into the 80 stores they had at the time."

That first significant deal had taken two years of salesmanship and negotiation, and would have exhausted a less determined company. "For those two years we were forever telling the bank it was going to come, it was going to come, and they continued to support us. With hindsight the manager took a real risk in supporting us, and if he had not done so we would not be here today," says Shazia. "Finally Waitrose came through, and then we got a deal with Tesco after that."

Expansion from there on was brisk. By 1988, having achieved sales of £400,000 by targeting the big chains' different depots across Britain one by one, Abel moved into a factory four times the size of their original block in Livingston. The breads were still being made by hand, and baked carefully in a tandoori oven. Asda followed Tesco as buyers, and Wazir continued to court Sainsbury and Marks & Spencer as potential clients, while continuing to supply the smaller convenience stores around Scotland and the north of England.

"By 1989 we had expanded the product beyond the basic nan and pakora. We were always looking for new ideas," says Wazir. "Shazia actually developed the garlic and coriander nan. No-one else had it, and yet it is so popular that even the Indian restaurants serve it now. Back then it was a new concept, and it really helped us."

The company also decided to "flow wrap" the breads, so that they were packaged in a similar way to biscuits. The breads came in colourful packaging adorned with Abel's brand logo, and the company marked different products in different colours. "So you could go into a supermarket and look at the usual dull and dreary packets of bread in polythene bags with plain black writing, before you were hit with our blue bag, or green or yellow bags for instance," points out Wazir. "That brought impulse buying, because people could not miss the packaging. Tesco picked up on that and after six months they had us making the bread for them and packaging it in under their label. Only our brand was on the shelves."'

The company was growing, from two to 20 employees, and then suddenly into a much bigger dimension. Shazia took on the training of new staff, relying as ever on instinct rather than management school skills. "We worked very hard so it was really a case of trying to lead by example. In those days we had people working for us who would not go home until the orders were complete - they would stay behind even to help get the vehicle loaded. They were all very dedicated."

She is proud that the growth itself was generated by the couple's decision to trust their own instincts. Abel's plan was to introduce at least one new product each year, and help expand the market by doing so. At one stage Livingston Development Corporation attempted to counsel them that moving from 3,000 to 12,500 square feet of operating space might be too big a step. "But we knew our trade and what we were doing, so we just insisted. In the end they helped us a great deal, especially with fitting-out work. We moved to the new place in Deans and took on a factoring company so that we did not have to increase borrowings. That really was instrumental in helping us achieve that goal."

The factor would pay 80 per cent of Abel's invoices, knowing that the company was dealing with "blue chip" clients such as Tesco and Sainsbury. This sort of arrangement helps growing companies avoid running huge overdrafts while waiting for payment on products already delivered.

During the five years to 1992, sales had jumped from £400,000 to £900,00, and then from £1.7m to £3.2m, and still further to £4.4m. Abel was beginning to attract the attention of the business press as much as it was from its new big customers. The Gallams, who eschewed publicity during their early years, became more confident, hired a public relations' consultant, and set about building their brand image in pursuit of more and more growth. It seemed everyone wanted to know about the Indian food company with the magic touch.

It was time to move again, into the ill-fated 40,000 square feet plant on Houstoun estate. Marks & Spencer was buying, as was the north of England supermarket chain Morrison. And all of their customers were placing regular orders for much bigger quantities. The British nan bread market had taken off, and the spoils were going to the company which had improved quality, challenged its early competitors, and used brand packaging as a means of attracting new consumers. All of this is classic brand management, especially, for the food sector, and yet it was developed by a couple who had not set foot inside a business school: this was entrepreneurism by instinct, and it was working well.

By 1993, just nine years after starting with little more than an idea and a production-line which consisted of a tandoori oven and a few tables, Abel was turning over £6m and had cornered 80 per cent of its market. Its turnover was increasing at around 40 per cent each year. The supermarkets loved the Gallams: they could do little wrong, and it seemed that consumers could not get enough of their innovative products.

"We really did not do any public relations or public marketing until that time, and that was a deliberate attempt to get plenty of customers under our belt without alerting the competition. We knew growth would slow down eventually, and that we should consolidate, so that was the basic plan," recalls Shazia. "Earlier we had ignored the outside advice that we should raise our profile, hiring PR people and so on, because we believed that would be a mistake, and we were right."

Since 1991, nearly half a dozen competitors have arrived on the UK scene, many of them copying Abel's business formula. Larger food manufacturers have also added Abel-type products to their existing lines in an effort to scoop up additional income from a high-growth line. Abel now produces sales brochures in English, French, and German, and there is demand for published recipes developed by Shazia herself.

"You have to react to market trends (in this sector), and your perception of where the market is, and what will happen next. Any strategic plan can never really be as far as three years ahead - you can make such an attempt but it never actually happens that way so you have to know how to react to change and to any threats around ," believes Shazia.

Wazir thinks Abel was helped by being small enough to make decisions quickly, unencumbered by the management hierarchy of bigger companies. That early introduction of garlic and coriander nan bread, an idea sparked by the then popularity of garlic baguettes in 1989, took fewer than six months to achieve, from the original idea to sending product to the market. "So instead of going through the manager, to the senior manager and so on, right up to the chairman, we were able to make decisions very quickly and bounce ideas off each other. Most management is really common sense."

Even today, with a new structure and external shareholders, Abel has a larger board, including an independent chairman, Scottish businessman Bill Marnoch, but a comparatively slim management structure: a key element in its decision making.

But of course there was one terrible event for which the Gallams could not have planned. During 1994-95 their sales had reached £8.4m and they were planning a new factory with the aim of boosting that figure to £30m by 1997-98: a massive ambition. The fire which destroyed Abel in 1995 destroyed that long-term strategy, and forced the couple to rebuild not only their self-confidence, but to find the personal reserves to start all over again.

"The break after the fire meant we lost quite a bit of market share, and gave competitors the opportunity to step in to take up the slack. We faced different challenges to those of the past, trying to win back sales and knowing that we will not achieve everything we had hoped for in terms of growth," says Shazia.

"Our new success will be based on developing the markets that we do win back, and creating totally new markets. Exporting is an important part of our strategy now."

It was with foreign sales in mind that the new company had "international" added to its former name. Shazia has introduced a Peshwari nan (with sultanas and apple sauce) as well as the wholewheat chapati and other breads such as the Mirch Masala Nan, which includes chillis. All of those new products require new skills, because of the broader range of ingredients: recipes have to be drawn up and tested, and production methods kept under rigorous review in order to maintain quality.

All along the couple have spurned expensive market research whenever they have planned new products. Instead they test out their ideas on friends and even people who work for them - "ordinary Joes" as Wazir describes them. He adds: "Instead of going out and spending time and money finding 100 people we already had people who could tell us what they thought."

The couple have used external consultants, such as Almond Design for their packaging, in areas where they acknowledge they do not have the necessary expertise. Shazia herself is attempting to devolve more responsibilities to other managers so that she can concentrate on developing company strategy and on that vital strength, introducing all-new products to the market.

Like many owner-managed businesses, the Gallams probably felt quite isolated during those years after starting up. Their focus was almost entirely on the company and its growth. When they moved into profit, their money was reinvested in new machinery, bigger premises, and hiring more employees. In addition, the Houstoun site was bought rather than rented: the realisation of a long-held dream for the couple.

Both admit that they experienced first shock, and then rushes of adrenalin, during the days and weeks following the blaze that had brought their lives to a standstill. The further blow of realising that no insurance money would be forthcoming (without a legal battle which could still go on for a lengthy period) had hardly sunk in when those vital offers of help began to arrive.

"The machinery we use is very specialised and expensive, yet we had manufacturers in Europe who were willing to rush equipment to us when we first thought of starting up on a temporary basis. They were even willing to divert machinery from other customers," says Wazir.

Shazia felt she had to find jobs for her former workforce as quickly as possible, although in the end only a handful have transferred from Livingston to Cumbernauld. Managers were sent around Scotland looking for new premises, talks continued with potential investors, and the company's architects agreed to work for free until a new financial package could be assembled in September - just three months after the blaze.

Andrew Hudson had been hired as Abel's finance director just before the fire, and arrived to find the Gallams' business in ruins. Yet he decided to leave his former company as planned and join the couple in their attempts to rebuild their operation. Although the Cumbernauld premises were a shell, constructed speculatively for a new investor, production commenced in November while offices were still being fitted out. An extension began in Spring of 1996.

"As the machinery was coming in one end and being commissioned we were cleaning up at the other. We had to have the place authorised by the major customers (including the supermarket chains) so we had to get the place spick and span and show them a full production run. I think they were amazed that we had got going so quickly," says Shazia. Sainsbury and Marks & Spencer placed orders quickly afterwards.

The couple mesh together well. Wazir worked hard in the early years to oversee the business as well as running affairs in the area for which has the greatest affinity, marketing. His was the company's public face, something he shares today with Shazia. Their conversation is peppered with gentle asides and mild jokes, underlining the unusual fact that here is a husband and wife who can work together successfully.

Shazia admits that the blaze, the destruction of a business in which she had spent most of her waking hours for many years, may have brought an ironic advantage. "The publicity that surrounded the fire has created a greater awareness out there. People are curious, and they want to try the product. And of course we found so many people who were willing to help us. Without them I do not think we would be here today."

She is a determined businesswoman, in demand for interviews, or to speak at business events. Significantly, she believes her success is important because she is a woman, rather than an Asian, and she shows a keen interest in encouraging more women to enter business and aim for the top.

Meanwhile, Shazia is intent on recreating the success for which she and Wazir - who says making money is no more important than the satisfaction wrought from achievement - had worked so hard, before fate threw down a gauntlet and challenged them to achieve their best all over again. There is little doubt they will succeed, and it is possible that their harsh experience will stand them in good stead in an increasingly competitive world.

Despite all that, despite the cheers and encouragement from investors, suppliers and customers, there is an unmistakable look in Shazia's eyes which signals that she wishes dearly that the nightmare of June 30th 1995 had never happened at all.

CHAPTER ELEVEN

From Tea to the Gentry to Jive about Java

They look like scientists, yet their "laboratory" is a nondescript factory building on Glasgow's industrial south side. There men in white coats seek perfection as they practise the magic art of roasting coffee and blending tea. In a nearby store room stand bulging sacks of coffee beans and chests full of imported tea, lending a great sense of tradition amid the bustle of the packaging area.

Meanwhile in the boardroom, the youthful managing director is enthusing about his company's latest pages on the Internet. A rich brew of text and graphics, it markets specialist coffees on the World Wide Web. His predecessors at Matthew Algie & Son may have discussed the finer details of shipping raw materials from halfway round the world, but David Williamson's ambitions are fixed on the new century which beckons. He is jiving about java, international style.

The fact that one of Glasgow's oldest surviving family companies was also among the first to launch its own Internet presence illustrates the youthful culture which has swept through the firm's Gorbals headquarters since the latest generation of management arrived.

The sixth generation is represented by 30-year-old David, a computer literate marketing whizz kid whose speech lapses occasionally into

Americanisms as he bubbles with enthusiasm about his future plans. He took over formally from his father Charles in January 1995. Both are direct descendants of the original Matthew Algie, a prominent Glasgow merchant who founded the company in 1864.

Algie passed the businesses to his daughter, Ann, who married a Williamson. At one crisis stage during the 1940s, the then boss, Grace Williamson, enlisted the help of a local businessman, Harald Grieve, who joined as managing director and later chairman. His son Harvey works alongside David Williamson as senior taster and buyer at the firm's unpretentious base on the site of the former Dixon's Blazes engineering works in the Gorbals.

The accountancy firm BDO Stoy Hayward estimates that just 24 per cent of family businesses survive the hand over to a second generation, and only 14 per cent make it to the third. One study of the sector blames the situation on "failure to manage the complex and emotion-laden issue of succession from one generation to the next".

The situation at Algie has been no different. Although the Williamsons have managed to achieve the hand-over successfully now for six generations, the going has not always been smooth. David and his father were determined that this time would be different.

In the company's post-war history, the first crunch came during the 1950s, and again in the 1970s: Charles says that business was only a matter of survival during both periods. Today, the company's youthful managing director pays tribute to his father for ensuring that the hand-over in late 1994 was done in as uncomplicated a way as possible. Father Charles remains chairman, "and I know I can turn to him for advice or support", adds David.

But first some history. The original Matthew Algie was a Glasgow merchant and grandee, who served as a Justice of the Peace and county councillor in Renfrewshire. His origins had been in Greenock, where as a local grocer he began importing tea and distributing it by the chest to local stores.

His business venture very nearly did not come off. In the 1850s, a local banker introduced him to a partner. As the company's own brief published history recalls: "Matthew Algie was a better judge of teas than partners". The busy new company was nearly strangled at birth by the partner's undisclosed previous debts. But rather than concede defeat, Algie paid off his by now former partner's creditors.

In gratitude, the creditors presented Algie with a tea service, "to testify their respect and admiration for sterling integrity and high principle evinced by him under circumstances of a particularly trying character". In 1864, Algie bought a tea-blending drum and restarted his operation in Glasgow.

A contemporary local journal, Glasgow and its Environs: A Literary, Commercial, and Social Review, written very much in the language of the time, remarked in 1891 that Mr Algie showed "a zealous regard for the intellectual welfare of youth" as a member of the Cathcart School Board. By this time Algie had been in business for 27 years.

The company then was one of numerous tea merchants, importers, and shippers. Tea dominated the imperial market, a reversal of the situation today, when coffee holds sway and has become by far the more popular beverage in the western world.

"From the commencement they have held facilities of resource only attainable by first-rate influence and capital, and largely to their active exertions may be attributed many of those gratifying commercial results whereby teas of genuine excellence have been brought within reach of all classes of the community", added the 1891 journal.

The company, which imported teas from India, China, Ceylon, and Japan, "devoted long and assiduous study to the many phases of blending, and the operations thereof they accomplish with the aid of a first rate modern mechanical plant", the Victorian commentator discovered.

"As connoisseurs of note, they have endeavoured to place upon the markets the most exquisite and fragrant blends of tea at a range of prices profitable to retailers and consumers alike; and they have done much to preserve the fine tone and character of the teas which those who have been long in the trade have pleasant recollections of.

"In these times of brisk tea trade competition it is especially gratifying to note the vitality and importance of a house so firmly established on a basis of honourable and straightforward trading, and we need only add that...Messrs Algie have few rivals."

The language is flowery Victoriana and slavishly uncritical, so much so that David Williamson jokes that "maybe Matthew wrote it himself". But it gives some idea of the scale and reputation of the business at the time. Then based in Ann Street, off Glasgow's Jamaica Street, near the Clyde, Algie imported tea, blended it, and exported cases of the blend overseas as well as servicing the significant local market of Glasgow, then the undisputed Second City of the British Empire.

One million people lived in Glasgow then, and neighbourhoods flourished. Algie's supplied local grocery stores with its own brands such as Kiosk, Aroma Tips, Garden Tea, Lily Bank, and Golden Tip. Some clients even demanded special blends to suit their own customers: one such was created for the well-to-do working class district of Maryhill on the city's north side.

The company competed with between 30 and 40 others throughout Scotland, but bought out some of them and watched others perish down through the generations. It became to the west of Scotland what Melrose's tea was to the east - a dominant local brand. The company moved into larger premises in Glasgow's Cadogan Street in 1930, before arriving in the Gorbals in 1964 in a 5,000 square foot base which has grown now to 50,000 square feet. Melrose's was taken over by Premier Brands, and the Edinburgh plant now produces herbal teas for the UK market.

In the 1950s, when the company was run by Grace Williamson, David's great-aunt, there was a crisis. Grace, the Scottish industry's only woman tea buyer for many years, had assumed control from her brother Thomas during the war. She had done enough for the company to survive rationing and shortage. But competition was increasing, and the major manufacturers were beginning to mass-produce tea. The company began to carry coffee on its books, but only as a supplier, at a time when coffee was becoming truly fashionable throughout Britain, partly as a result of the post-war influence of America and because people had become more used to visiting mainland Europe on holiday or business.

The one important cause in the decline of tea was Britain's austere post-war period. Rationing continued: customers had to register with a supplier whose statutory duty was to sell them less than the quantities they sought. The Empire - and the tea plantations of the Indian sub-continent - was fragmenting. The company and many of its competitors stagnated, and then it was hurt by what became known famously within the sector as the Tea Market Crash of 1954.

Tea prices climbed as rationing ended, but crashed from six shillings and sixpence per pound to just three shillings and four pence (the equivalent of falling from 33p to 17p today). Meanwhile, UK brands were being marketed aggressively, and the early multiples were starting to develop their buying power. Grace had by then recruited the help of businessman Harald Grieve as managing director, and the Grieve family retains 48 per cent of the company as a result.

Harald's company, Polson Deacon & Webb was small, but offered Algie's an entree into the growing coffee market. More important to the acquisition was Harald himself, who ran the company until his retirement in the 1980s. Charles was sales manager and had been a willing understudy since joining the company at the age of 19 in 1954.

"Without Harald we would not have had a business. He could read the tea and coffee market better than anyone. And that more than anything else was important to the company's survival," points out Charles. "Plus the age gap between us is about 17 years, so it was good when it came to handing over."

Charles Williamson arrived at the company, as his son was to do so much later on, full of enthusiasm and ideas. But throughout the 1960s and 1970s the company remained very small, a survivor of the supermarket boom which had left many local competitors by the wayside. Algie had bought two or three former rivals along the way, but in the late 1970s still employed fewer than 40 people.

The big breakthrough was to come during a summer visit to Vancouver. Charles made a point, wherever he was on holiday or business, to look up the local telephone directory and find out who was in the coffee and tea business. He paid a routine call on a Vancouver company, Dickson's, and saw that they were supplying and maintaining coffee machines as well as the coffee itself: a very different system from that traditionally employed in Britain.

The British hotel trade particularly had long depended on a central source of brewed coffee. "Nearly every big hotel included a still-room, fed by a great big boiler. They had huge numbers of staff rolling in at 6am to prepare maybe 400 breakfasts, and there was very little quality control," explains Charles. "And since the coffee suppliers had no control over the equipment, there was a gap in consistency of service and supply."

Charles and Harald knew they were on the brink of a big opportunity. They imported smaller, more portable coffee-making machines, adapted them, and recruited their own engineering support team when they acquired a small Edinburgh firm whose task it had been to service milk and fruit-juice dispensers in company canteens. New skills had to be learned, but the dividend for Algie was considerable.

"It is accepted practice now, but it was extremely unusual in Britain back then," says David. "My father and Harald telephoned round every office and company they could think of: people they knew such as lawyers and insurance brokers and so on. It soon became apparent that the formula would work with caterers as well."

The simple innovation picked up almost casually in Vancouver was to transform the coffee-buying habits of companies and hotel groups back home. For years, the simple task for a company of laying on coffee for staff and clients involved two entirely separate buying decisions: first in buying a coffee machine and secondly, the coffee to go into. Price was the only dictating factor, with the consequence that standards could be extremely low.

Managers at Matthew Algie knew they were on to something, although they may not have guessed just how important the coffee market was to become. By the early 1980s they had a clear strategy, helped by winning contracts from noted Scottish hotels such as Gleneagles and Crieff Hydro.

An office was opened in Kensington, west London, staffed with an engineer who could provide support to new customers in the capital. A contract with Ladbroke Hotels promised a break into the UK hotels market, helped by word of mouth recommendations, especially from Scottish expatriates. "You tend to find that the average food and beverages manager will move around the different hotel groups, and he will take his suppliers with him, especially if he is impressed with the service," explains David. His father remembers that at first those potential customers he contacted were not interested in his carefully-rehearsed pitch about being an independent Scottish company offering a new idea. "It was the service side that was vital. They just wanted to know the deal. That was it," he adds.

The development was to benefit David when it came time for him to take over. Algie's had developed as a more diverse business, dominated by the booming coffee machine sector. "The company was not doing something unique, but certainly something different. The formula became well established. We have a lot of machines, and a wide variety of types depending on the task they are needed for," says David. "The task in hotels is to serve up 400 coffees in a 20 minute period, say during a hotel conference or some kind of function as well as meals. We brought the answer to that with those machines.

"We were innovative and enthusiastic, and the company benefited from the boom of the mid to late 1980s. We built up a number of big clients, and we work hard at keeping them."

When Charles helped move the company base to the Gorbals in 1964, Algie's staff numbered just 12. Today the extended factory and warehouse on Dixons' Blazes industrial estate houses 110 staff, working round the clock on shifts to supply hotels, businesses, and the supermarket chains with specially blended teas and roasted coffees. David - who worked for the company twice before taking over from his father - wants to build on that success, principally by helping to expand the market itself, as public tastes continue to develop, especially in the case of coffee.

Like so many children of business families, David visited the Gorbals site regularly and helped pack the tea from the age of eight, in 1974. The family - he has two sisters, both of whose share holdings were bought out at a later stage - lived, ate and breathed in the business environment. They were steeped in it. The dinner table at home witnessed regular debates about Algie's progress.

"I was a typical middle-class rebel in my late teens. I left home, wanting nothing to do with the business, and got an honours degree in economics at Edinburgh University. I looked at other job opportunities, wanting to get out and do things for myself, and on my own," he recalls.

However, after graduation, David did return to the company, working in London, where he helped set up a new depot, including offices and a showroom in Wembley, north London. He spent a further 18 months as a management trainee, packing tea chests and loading up for deliveries alongside the workforce. "I did all the jobs throughout the business. That is the only way to do it: you have to gain people's respect at every level of the company."

David believed that his skills lay in marketing. But he was not ready yet to return to work with his father. Although their relationship was always amicable, they had their differences about David's role. Looking back, he believes now his father was grooming him to take over, but attempting at the same time to ensure that he was aware of every area of the business, and the potential pitfalls of trying to "run before you can walk".

The sixth generation had to wait to take over. Charles decided he would step down at 60 - unusually for the head of a family business, he stuck to the plan - and clearly David would have to return to the company before then. But the details of the hand-over remained unclear, because David was still attempting to find his way in the commercial world. He knew that he needed experience.

The younger Williamson had married his university sweetheart, Lynn, and started a family. They now have three sons.

"I was drawn to marketing at that time. The company had no defined image: it sent out several varying messages at the same time. Marketing had not been accepted into the company's business philosophy.

"My relationship with my father was off and on, and has certainly improved since he retired. We have always argued about everything, but we do agree on strategy and direction. I joined again in 1987 as marketing manager (this at the age of 21), but there was some tension. We would tend to agree on a general point, but then there would be a big argument about the colour of a particular machine, for instance.

"I was prepared to stand up to him, and I think he liked that. He encouraged me to speak my mind. After all I have been disagreeing with him since I was 11."

David made a complete break, and joined Cumbernauld Theatre in 1989. He remembers the period as "brilliant fun", essentially because of the very different nature of the business, and because of the opportunities for learning something completely new to him. He moved on to become marketing and press publicity chief for Glasgow's major arts festival, Mayfest. "I could see a career in the arts looming!" he laughs.

The wanderer returned in 1991, and Charles signalled his intention that he would retire in 1994. "He stuck to that, and I was very pleased about it. I was confident in my abilities, and became managing director at 28. I try to ask for Dad's advice before he offers it. He enjoyed his last couple of years because I was able to take over some of the work, so there was pressure there, but it was a positive kind of pressure."

The business is four times the size it was a decade ago, in terms of sales and profitability, and turnover has doubled to around £10m in the past five years. "I want to do this for the family, and also to know that I can do it," says David firmly.

Charles confirms that the two did not get on comfortably prior to his decision to stand down. "Nearly 40 years in a business is long enough for anybody. David was able but becoming increasingly frustrated. Having made the decision I must admit the last 18 months were difficult for me. I was never any good at delegating, although in the end I found it remarkably easy."

He devotes more time to his pastime of sailing on Scotland's west coast, and chairs the public-private sector Gorbals Initiative, which attempts to improve the district's faltering economy. As Algie's chairman he is available to David if necessary, but confines himself usually to checking the figures each month. "David has a very sharp mind. I remember that in the business I did not have to tell him anything twice. And he is not the type of young man who just wants to have a Ferrari," says the chairman, who adds that his respect for his son has risen since the hand-over.

Charles believes he was fortunate in that, having taken advantage of the changes in personal pension rules, he was able to prepare himself for financial security in retirement. "I have seen many other companies come to grief eventually because people have stayed on too long just to maintain their income," he adds. "And very often the next generation were prevented from taking over, even though they were ready to do so."

The company's independence remains important, so much so that its management spent more than £2m buying out peripheral shareholders a few years ago, to ensure that equity remained within the management team. Charles, David, and Harvey Grieve own Algie outright today. "There were only seven peripheral shareholders involved, but as years go by shares are passed on, and we could have ended up with many more. That can mean death to an independent company," believes Charles.

The company has received an "endless" stream of takeover inquiries over the years, and the abrupt changes within its sector during the last 50 years has left it among just four companies operating in Britain: the difference being that Algie is the only one to be independently owned and British.

There is a friendly atmosphere inside the deceptively nondescript looking Algie headquarters. The key areas include tea blending and packaging, coffee machine storage and servicing, and the vital coffee roasting area. A small team led by Harvey Grieve supervise the tasting and preparation of coffee. Marketing-minded David wants to cash in on the booming world taste in coffee, an enthusiasm for which appears to know no bounds for modern consumers.

He takes his inspiration from the booming American north-west. In and around Seattle, Washington, and Portland, Oregon - themselves fashionable places of the 1990s - coffee is "in". Algie is among several European players trying to broaden its share of the market by emulating the American trend.

At the heart of the marketing campaign is an acknowledgment of the 1990s' "coffee culture". Consumers are no longer satisfied with a jar of instant coffee: they have become used to being served espresso and cappuccino, and even to making quality beverages of that kind in their own homes. Many modern kitchens include a cafetiere or espresso maker, superseding the coffee percolator, which was once seen as a luxury item.

Algie has been well-established in the catering market for many years, and includes upmarket clients such as The Ritz Hotel in London as well as the Hilton chain, Harrods, and Sir Terence Conran's restaurants. It supplies machines on a "gentlemen's agreement" basis, relying on the downstream trade in supplying the coffee itself.

But there are 10,000 speciality coffee outlets in the US. TV sitcoms like "Ellen" and "Friends" regularly include scenes which centre on the characters' local coffee bars. The fashion spread quickly to the UK, particularly in areas like London's Soho and Covent Garden. Consumers are just as likely to request a Coffee Latte, Macchiatto or Ristretto as they are to accept a plain old cup of coffee.

Williamson has visited the US regularly and noted the changing trends, just as his father had spotted the potential for sales to offices and other places of work back in the 1970s. Today American suppliers offer a plethora of flavourings and extras - such as banana, cinnamon, liquorice, nutmeg, and chocolate fudge - to meet the new demand for more and more exotic coffees.

The new managing director explains the situation in his boardroom, which is redolent with the aroma of fine coffee. Across from his place stands a row of coffee machines with strange names like Bunnomatic. Occasionally he leaps from his seat to one of them to whip up a new java brew for tasting. He bubbles with enthusiasm when he explains the finer points of this flavour or that coffee-making technique.

David and his colleagues will meet regularly to discuss the quality of the "crema" - the light layer of bubbles - at the top of an espresso. Perhaps the fact that the company remains close-knit, and its management team thin in numbers, helps everyone involved to remember that their product is what matters. In this Glasgow company senior management cannot escape the aroma from the production floor, and that clearly helps when it comes to providing the business with its focus.

The priority now is to develop an integrated coffee service. Algie will train a client's staff on the making of speciality coffees at their own "school", as well as providing the machines, a 24-hour engineering call-out service, marketing support, and that essential ingredient, the coffee itself.

There is a particularly obvious commercial attraction in selling speciality coffees: the mark-up. Retailers can take eight basic coffees, and use an array of flavourings to offer hundreds of variations. Premium coffee, made at a cost of just 10p, can be sold for up to £2 a time. Since Williamson introduced the package, he says 70 per cent of his traditional "cappuccino and espresso" customers have shown interest.

The company has a database which lists an incredible 500 coffee variations. In true 1990s' style, Williamson plans to make many of them available on the

Internet, via his company's World Wide Web pages. He is a technophile, who confesses to judging people by whether they use an Apple Mac or an IBM-compatible PC: Williamson has Macs, a computer associated usually with creativity, being particularly strong in the publishing and education markets.

Another innovation, based on another idea imported from North America, is the coffee cart. Williamson teamed up with Glasgow businessman Carlo Ventisei to provide Scotland's first "espresso cart" in the city's St Enoch shopping centre. Algie provides the automatic machine which creates those eight basic coffees, including Mocha and Latte, at the touch of a button.

The cart includes a fridge, lighting system, and sink, complete with a water heater and tank. Williamson believes that "dead areas", such as hotel lobbies, shopping precincts, railway stations, museums, offices, and airports, could be revitalised as profit-making centres with the simply-constructed carts. He wants to franchise the idea, reasoning that businesses of all sizes may be attracted by the relatively low cost of participation.

As a parallel, there are more than 10,000 such carts in the US, 300 of them in Seattle alone: Williamson believes that, apart from the fact that Seattle has become "fashionable" as the home of grunge music and the software giant Microsoft, its climate is more like that of Britain. "It tends to be cold and wet, and so coffee is more popular there than other American favourites such as frozen yoghurt," he adds.

"It is very hard to predict the likely demand for speciality coffee in the UK over the next few years, but in the US it has become a billion dollar industry with its own language, magazines, trade shows and support industries. I think that now is the time for caterers to radically rethink their approach to coffee selections," says David.

The heavy American influence has indeed produced a speciality coffee "language". An expert espresso waiter or retailer is known as a "barista", while "double cupping" is the phrase given to describe the practice of placing a take away cup of hot coffee inside a second cup in order to protect the drinker's hands from burning. A whipless coffee is one without whipped cream, while coffee-drinkers are known to ask for some "skinny", or semi-skimmed milk. Ever enterprising, Algie has supplied a list of the new terms on the back of a free guide.

Back at base, however, the priority remains to maintain the company's quality image in roasting and bagging its own beans. Coffee beans are ground in order to produce a larger surface area on which water can act. But any gas is expelled within five hours of grinding, which is why "fresh ground coffee" is vacuum packed to retain its freshness.

"We buy the raw beans, roast and pack them for supply. Our business is in futures, to the extent that we buy through brokers in London who deal in turn with others in New York. We do resist the temptation to speculate," explains

David.

"We buy tea as an option through brokers. The difference between tea and coffee is that the skill in tea is in buying the right quality before blending it. Coffee quality depends on what we do when it arrives here.

"Coffee is a highly complicated product. Apart from sitting around examining the crema of an espresso, we have to think about how it is presented and marketed. That was why we looked at America in the first place.

"People wanted to see coffee in a new light. The quality of coffee in American offices and hotels, just like here, was sometimes terrible. It was like sock juice. But the consumers changed all that. With speciality coffees it is all about putting cinnamon on top of a cappuccino instead of chocolate, or presenting an espresso in a 'shot glass' instead of a cup."

David Williamson clearly holds the company whose management he has inherited in great esteem. His infectious enthusiasm has already made a mark. During his first year in charge, the supermarket giant Safeway named Matthew Algie & Co as its Scottish Supplier of the Year. Williamson has a similarly close relationship with Tesco, which became an important local player after its acquisition of Scotland's last major independent chain, Dundee-based William Low.

So who inspires him? "Sir Terence Conran is a good example of someone with vision, and someone who does not compromise in pursuit of his goals. I like that," reflected David.

"The company is fiercely independent and committed to remaining so. I think I and my father feel a debt of gratitude to previous generations: we want to continue down the line. I do this for myself, but I also just see this as my time with the company, which will hopefully pass on to another generation in time." David and Lynn have three sons, all far too young to be considering their careers so far.

"All of that is great motivation. There is so much scope for further development. I really am convinced that this company will certainly satisfy my personal ambitions. For example, if you want to be broker, manufacturer, retailer, or whatever, you can try it," points out David.

"In a family business you spend your time with customers, and not just City people or shareholders. You can be different: you do not have to conform. And I like that idea too."

CHAPTER TWELVE

A Transition Success

When Brian Hall reached 50, he had been running his own successful graphics design company in Edinburgh for a decade but was becoming increasingly frustrated as the recession continued and competition became increasingly cut-throat.

Business had been brisk as Brian lived out his dream of self employment, having developed his skills carefully in order to strike out on his own. His enthusiasm and ideas kept things buoyant until recession came in the late 1980s. The change might have forced weaker firms to sell out or change direction. Brian's good fortune was that he had his family around him to take over the day to day running of his business.

Brian himself had waited until he was 40 before taking the big step into self-employment. An accomplished designer and manager with two leading Edinburgh printing and stationery firms, he had measured the market carefully before deciding with his wife Pamela and a business partner to launch Teviot Design.

It was 1983, and the concept of design was just then beginning to be recognised as important by corporate clients. British companies had long been criticised for under-estimating the value of good design, not just in products, but in the preparation of sales brochures and presentations as well as marketing literature and other materials. The concept of a developed corporate image - now a prerequisite for businesses and public organisations - remained vague for all but the most imaginative firms.

All that was changing. Deregulation was looming in the financial services market, and Scotland's major banks and insurance companies were beginning to become aware of the fact that as competition hotted up they would have to produce literature which would be attractive and accessible to their potential customers. Brian Hall intended to press that message home.

He obtained a £20,000 loan, rented a tiny office in Edinburgh's Cumberland Street Lane, so dingy that fungus seeped through the floor and ruined the carpets, and began operations. "The clients who said they would come with me did so. That was the big challenge. It was quite scary," recalls Brian.

Everything had been carefully planned. Even the name of the company was selected for its Edinburgh connotations, its sense of integrity - "a solid name with a 't' at either end", explains Brian - and its apparent familiarity. Brian reasoned that much of his business might come from companies managed by alumni of Edinburgh University, whose great social rendezvous is in the city's Teviot Row. He thought the name might bring back warm memories for them.

A keen painter and amateur artist, Brian had developed a variety of skills while creating a design studio for George Waterston's stationery business, and then as a director of McDonald's printers. "I always enjoyed the creative side most. Looking back I suppose that deep in my subconsciousness I was collecting all the skills I would need for my own business. I must have been doing that, although I did not have the focus at the time. My aim was simply to have the best graphics design studio in Edinburgh."

He and Pamela had done freelance business from home for several years, with the permission of Brian's employers, so they had a distinct feel for the market already. Design was in demand, and there were few studios in Scotland capable of attacking the business properly.

He admits to having been very cautious during the year prior to setting up Teviot with the help of a designer friend, Julian Draper. Apart from drawing up estimates of monthly cash-flow, Brian went to unusual lengths to check the market: "There were a couple of other design houses already in Edinburgh and I even went round and looked at their homes and the sort of cars they were driving to try and work out what sort of incomes they had."

The market was good to Teviot in the early years, so much so that turnover had reached a peak of £1.3m by 1990. "The major thing was that the financial institutions had always thought they could sell what they wanted to sell by just typing out things on rubbishy notepaper and so on. It was years before they tackled serious design."

His first clients included the Life Association of Scotland, the defence electronics giant Ferranti, and the shipping firm Ben Line. Within three years Brian had snapped up work from Scotland's biggest company, the insurer

Standard Life, whose orders quickly came to represent 70 per cent of Teviot's income. Other clients, including big insurers like Scottish Amicable and Scottish Widows, quickly followed. Teviot was an unsung success story in Edinburgh, having relied upon word of mouth for business.

Then recession came. Teviot survived: in fact it has never gone into the red. But Brian Hall became increasingly under stress as he struggled to hang on to his clients and maintain earnings. Where once there had been just three design companies in the city, there were now more than 50. Technology had changed the work itself, and the competition was tougher, especially since most potential clients had introduced the theory of competitive tendering to their contracts processes. One key problem was in managing individual projects so that they remained within the original cost estimates. Brian, more of a creative person than a manager, was being forced to cope with new personal demands.

Brian's experience makes for a familiar story. A small specialist service sector operator gets fat on some lucrative work from a few comparatively wealthy clients. Then things go wrong, and usually quickly. Growth stops and sales go into reverse. In other circumstances Brian could have cut back operations and hoped for the best. Or he might have sold out to a competitor and decided to retire early.

None of those options were considered. The main reason was that by 1991 Brian, then 48, was employing his own son and daughter, Craig, then 22, and Jane, just 18 months younger, and a very determined pair indeed. Their roles within the company - Craig in production and Jane in marketing - were becoming increasingly important as they learned their trade. The concepts of making formal pitches for work or using technology to reduce costs were not unusual to them: their careers had begun in that modern, more competitive environment anyway.

Jane had joined straight from Currie High School in 1987, "temping" at first as the Teviot receptionist, and developing her natural flair for marketing. Craig arrived a year later after qualifying in biochemistry at Edinburgh University; having been offered a job with the pharmaceutical giant Glaxo in Middlesex, he decided a scientific career was not for him, and joined his father's firm as a production assistant.

Although times were tougher and profits more difficult to come by, the flow of business continued to strengthen and sources of income became more diverse. Teviot was to win two Scottish Advertising Awards for "best overall design" and "best corporate brochure" in 1993, to add to other prizes in London and San Francisco. The firm's new premises in Dublin Street Lane were extended by knocking through the wall to take in a neighbouring flat. But Brian remained frustrated about the market place and about the administrative side of the business. By 1991 the children were making their mark, amid several personnel changes. Jane became worried about the stress being suffered by her father. Craig was "champing at the bit", in his own words, to play a more senior role, and perhaps even to take over the management of the business itself.

The history of family businesses is littered with internal rivalries and botched attempts to transfer management from the first generation to the second. Many such companies actually fail at that crucial point and wind up bust. Teviot's experience is a model in achieving transition.

Julian Draper had moved on some years previously, and Brian's wife Pamela worked only from home. Brian began to hanker after developing his skills in abstract painting, having had two successful local exhibitions of his work, and while his enthusiasm for the business was as high as ever, he was enjoying it less and less.

The reason lay partly in the recent history of the design sector. The great innovation of the 1980s was the arrival of the Apple Macintosh computer. Its intuitive design was a boon to graphics artists, and it quickly became a standard feature of studios, as well as becoming dominant in the education and publishing sectors. Teviot quickly adopted the new medium and developed its skills, initially to the company's enormous benefit.

"Many designers were slow to appreciate the massive difference the Apple Mac could make. It was a great tool which increased the amount of artwork you could do. You still had to get the concept and ideas for a design down using brain and paper, but the Mac allowed you to get variations on those original ideas very quickly," says Brian.

But the machine which proved such a boon brought along an unexpected down-side for Teviot. Its ease of use encouraged many more people to set up design studios. And clients themselves thought the computer would allow them to save money by moving design work "in house". Brian remembers some clients noting the equipment he had in his studio, and then returning to their head offices to order the same machines, despite their lack of appropriate design skills. Teviot remained profitable, but sales had declined by nearly 40 per cent to less than £800,000.

Where Brian's strength was in ideas, Craig was fascinated by process, and by computers. He had used an early Mac during a university research project, and his experience on the production side at Teviot fired his enthusiasm. "Dad is not good with figures. And for me spreadsheets and databases are not a problem, in fact I just loved working with them. I could see him getting bogged down in all that, and at the same time I was getting more frustrated because I knew I could sort things out," says Craig.

Father and children sit together in Dublin Street Lane today and recall good-humouredly how the decision to begin Teviot's management succession came together. "We had blow-ups every two to three months. It became so regular I almost started putting it in my diary," jokes Brian. "We laugh now but it was not all so funny at the time," points out Craig. "We pushed Dad to make the decision because it was all getting more cut-throat and he found it more and more stressful," remembers Jane.

The youngsters felt they held the key to Teviot's future. Jane, uninhibited by the cultural change which had imposed new competitive pressures in many commercial sectors by the early 1990s, developed her ability to sniff out new business and pitch successfully for contracts. Her brother Craig, happier with the practical side of management, believes Jane is more like their father: "They are both very good at seeing the big picture. I am more fascinated by the actual running of the business."

With his computer expertise and more developed knowledge of production needs, Craig set about reducing costs and keeping a more accurate account of the company's activities. His priority was to ensure that individual jobs came in within their original budgets. Brian, in his first clear acceptance of the notion that he should be beginning to hand over the business while still quite young himself, agreed to spend Fridays at home. "It was never at the stage where I was losing sleep at night: it never was that bad. But there was a massive change in the market place. Clients realised that by forcing studios to pitch for work, they could hear ideas from four different companies, and then just pick the ones they liked for free," he says. "It was all very different from my experience."

The company realised that, while it enjoyed a great deal of goodwill and some prestige with its clients, especially in the financial services sector, its long-standing reliance on "word of mouth" referrals meant that its general profile was low. Craig decided the firm needed more publicity, and a generally higher profile, to reach potential clients who may not have heard of Teviot.

Craig and Jane divided their duties across the firm's range of activities. With their father's help - he still manages some key accounts from home - they increased the spread of clients to 20, and began to develop new markets, such as design for the World Wide Web, a sector of business which is predicted to soar in the years ahead.

The Web is growing haphazardly and at a massive rate, with tens of thousands of companies now establishing "home pages" for their customers. Specialist companies like Teviot argue that, although the medium is different, design has an added importance on the Web, in order that a company's presence there is attractive, easy to navigate, and carries useful information. Craig has undertaken to train staff in the additional technical skills demanded by the Web, and Teviot has started to market "Web authoring services" to clients like the Speyside food giant W.A. Baxter.

Brian's next big step was to move office. "I realised that I could not take my hands off the work if I was still physically in the same position. I had the biggest office in the building and I actually had to move out of it. That took me a few months, but Craig and Jane were quite supportive. They did not push me." He moved to a smaller office in the city centre studio, and then a shared one, before moving to a more personal base converted from the attic of the family home in Balerno, keeping in touch with a telephone link which allows clients such as Scottish Power to contact him directly via the Teviot office switchboard.

Five years after making that decision, Brian keeps in touch with Teviot frequently, but mainly on strategic issues, or to advise on staff matters such as salaries and bonuses. He and his children hold regular "vision meetings" with senior staff and an external adviser, Neil Aiston, a former Royal Bank of Scotland executive who gave Brian some valuable advice during Teviot's early days. "When I first considered setting up Neil advised me to work out the worst possible situation, and adding that if I thought I could survive that, then I could survive anything," Brian recalls. Brian tries to play a similar role for Craig and Jane, providing moral support whenever necessary.

Other key figures, outside the family group, include Julie Ainsley, an experienced design consultant now based in Leeds, and Kate Laing, the company's head of design in Edinburgh. Paul Dilger, a former strategic marketing specialist in the United States and with Whitbread and Royal Insurance, is now an associate director.

The client list includes a healthy spread of Scottish companies and local authorities, including the software developer McQueen, Lanarkshire engineering company Motherwell Bridge, Motorola, the Royal Bank of Scotland, and property consultants Ryden. The move into the north of England, via Julie Ainsley's operation in Leeds, is an important signal of Teviot's ambition to find new work beyond its traditional Scottish market. Craig is also following up potential leads overseas.

"When you build a business and prepare to hand it over you have to be very sure that you could jump in and grab the reins if the horse has gone off the road and into a ditch. That was important when the children were still learning the business, but that stage is long past," reflects Brian. "I know now that I could walk out of the door and that if I did not come back for two or three years things would still be OK."

This has always been a close family. As children, Craig and Jane joined their parents on regular campaign holidays around Britain. Craig remembers helping his father restore a two-man canoe one summer. The children, being so close in ages, tend to complement each other well. When brother and sister found themselves discussing the succession more often, and worrying about their father's stress levels, Jane kept in touch with her mother to hear her views on the situation.

They agree that there were few real periods of conflict, simply because the family has always been open with each other and very supportive. "At first I was very conscious of being the boss's son. I remember we had a Christmas cheese and wine party in the office, and he told me to call him Brian and not Dad. Of course within a few minutes I called out 'Dad!' to him without thinking. It was hard to wipe out 21 years just like that," laughs Craig.

Apart from the regular strategic meetings, Craig has settled into his role as managing director by introducing new technology and new production practices, as well as regular staff appraisals. The family feel they have now recruited a more highly qualified team of people, as well as branching out recently in Leeds. Maintaining the family connection, Jane's husband Douglas MacDowall, a career in recruitment, car sales and hotel management behind him, has joined Teviot to take charge of business development.

Jane says the four held regular meetings at the family home prior to the full transition. She and Craig had attended seminars on family businesses and were acutely aware of the potential pitfalls of transferring control between first and second generations. "I think being a close family helped. Craig slotted into his role automatically. We still meet on a Sunday night over a Chinese takeaway and the only rule is that we do not discuss the business," she adds.

"We do not particularly want to become huge, and risk losing control. It is a family business and will always remains so." Jane and Craig took over the Teviot shareholdings once the management transition was complete.

Brian remains an important figure within Teviot. But his increased free time allows him to plan ahead and reflect on the company's progress since 1983. "I would like to think I am still there to answer questions where necessary. Obviously as the business changes and the market place continues to change, my ability to do that will be reduced, but I do still get very excited about our long term goals and future role," believes Brian.

"I just love to talk with the others about the way paper is not going to be used in future, and whether catalogues are going to be on the Web rather than in print. It is very exciting to know how involved we are in computing technology and how devoted we are becoming to the Internet now. I can get excited just looking forward to these developments even if I am not directly involved."

This has been a model handover, but all three know there have been hurdles to clear. Craig and Jane acknowledge that they are still relatively young, but then again their father's comparative youth means that the transition was not forced upon them, as is so often the case with family businesses. "I like to be part of the vision. But I still find it difficult to keep my hands off the business. That is inevitable as it is more like a weaning-off process," adds Brian.

"The essence of the transition has been that it is a gradual process. If you were working with a colleague rather than a relative then they would need to know exactly what you were doing, and when. But there is a great trust within any family business, and that helps."

CHAPTER THIRTEEN

Falkirk's Unlikely Press Baron

"**C**hancers," says Fred Johnston when asked to describe some of his predecessors at the head of what is now one of Britain's biggest independent local newspaper companies. "A succession of rogues and hell-raisers."

He is being mischievous. The history of Johnston Press is littered with the memories of ancestors whose role was rather unusual. One ran a Leith chandlery, and fled to Australia to escape his creditors when it went bust. Another Johnston forebear was involved in the last great North American Indian uprisings: quite what his role was, no-one is sure, but it appears to have been unsavoury. "He came back and made a real arse-up of the Falkirk Herald," says Fred in typical no-nonsense terms. Nevertheless, this company has survived and prospered for most of its two centuries in operation, to become one of Britain's biggest independent newspaper groups.

Times had changed for the better in 1882, when the current chairman's great-uncle Fred - whose portrait takes pride of place in the boardroom of Johnston's unpretentious Edinburgh headquarters - took over the business, a printing interest whose flagship was, and remains, the Falkirk Herald title. In fact, until the early 1980s, this was a quintessential family business owning and operating more than 20 Scottish weekly newspapers such as the Herald,

Ayr Advertiser Oban Times, and Fife Free Press.

But it had expanded quickly, and by 1988 - more than 200 years after its foundation - Johnston Press became a public company. Today the family's collective shareholding amounts to less than 30 per cent of the total, as successive rights' issues have been made to investors and the City in order to fund more and greater expansion.

Today, having floated when sales reached £30m, Johnston Press turns over £100m a year. A recent ambitious takeover of a string of local papers from the East Anglian based EMAP group in 1996 has virtually doubled that figure to £200m. Johnston Press owns no less than 146 newspapers now, from Kirkcaldy to the Isle of Man, and from Eastbourne to Halifax: despite the firm's strong Scottish roots, just 16 of those papers are north of the Border, although these include some of the company's longest-established titles. City analysts, normally cautious about the newspaper publishing sector, love the company which has developed a knack of maintaining editorial integrity whilst slashing costs and overheads in each of its acquisitions.

The family's origins can be traced back to 1767 when Patrick Mair began a printing and pamphlet publishing business in Falkirk. His daughter married a local printer, Thomas Johnston, Fred's great-great grandfather. Thomas' son Archibald took over in 1831, taking over the Falkirk Herald in 1846, and handing over to his son Fred 51 years later. It was only then that the business became stable once more - allowing for the behaviour of those earlier "chancers and rogues".

Old Fred remained in control, primarily as the Falkirk Herald publisher, for more than half a century, and his place was taken by his nephew Fred - the current chairman's father - in 1936.

It was into this environment that the young Fred Johnston arrived in 1962, aged 26. He had already become something of a "lad o' pairts", having spent his National Service with the Black Watch, and then volunteering to join the King's African Rifles in Kenya during the Mau-Mau rebellion, and later in Uganda. He returned to New College, Oxford, to read modern history, before joining the Liverpool Evening Echo as a trainee journalist, and then graduating to its morning sister title, the Post.

From there young Fred joined the London Times in 1960, not as a journalist this time but as a manager, assistant company secretary when "The Thunderer", as the paper was known affectionately, was still in the hands of the Astor family.

He returned to the fold primarily to help run the business, his father having apparently lost any keen interest. "My father was there only four days a week, and on some of those days he arrived very late and would go out immediately to have lunch with his cronies in a local bar called Mathieson's Rest," remarks Fred. "He tended to leave the business to run itself. And of course it was a lot smaller then.

"I had married, and our first son had been born. My London lifestyle had been based on two salaries, and really I could not stay there. I had been offered promotion at The Times, but my father told me that his print works' manager had died, and that I could have his cottage in Falkirk for £54 a year rent. I had been paying £6 a week in London, and so I came home."

By this time the Falkirk Herald had been joined by the Linlithgowshire Journal and other local titles such as the Grangemouth Advertiser. In local newspaper terms, this was still rather small beer. The young Johnston fell quickly into league with his father's general manager, a war veteran and former prisoner of the Japanese, Tom McGowran, a man who became celebrated as a manager of vision within Scottish local newspaper circles. Now retired, he spent more than three years as a Japanese prisoner of war, having endured forced labour on the notorious Burma to Siam railway line.

McGowran had begun his newspaper career with The Scotsman, moving to the Falkirk company prior to the war. Captured in Singapore in 1942, he was released only at the end of the war in 1945, and immediately rejoined the business. He had gradually taken over its day to day management during the intervening years before young Fred arrived.

"We were kindred spirits. We shared the same vision. I had been offered the post of personal assistant to the managing director at The Times, and that would have been a route to the top. So I had thought long and hard before deciding to return to Scotland," points out Fred.

"I was ambitious. Then I teamed up with Tom and between us we persuaded my father to do many things that he would not have done in the past, such as bidding for other newspapers. I suppose Tom had always really wanted to get things into gear, and my arrival helped him get his way."

This was a very competitive market. While the "national" Scottish newspapers - such as the Express, Mail and Record - indulged in pitched battles for advertising and story exclusives, the local variety were no slouches either. Although the majority of local weekly titles remained in private ownership - often shares were spread across families who had inherited the business from their founders - there were aggressive players buying up newspapers across the country.

In 1963 Johnston and McGowran had got wind that their company's great rival, the Glasgow based George Outram & Co., was planning a new title to serve the growing "Glasgow overspill" population of Cumbernauld new town, a growth area which both companies wanted to dominate. Outram had already launched a similar paper in East Kilbride new town. The Glasgow-based company was planning to present its paper as an edition of the Airdrie and Coatbridge Advertiser, and named it the Cumbernauld Courier. Suddenly Johnston and McGowran saw the opportunity for which they had been looking, and launched a rival newspaper service, the Cumbernauld News.

"We went to see the manager of the ABC picture house in Riddrie, near Stepps. We offered him an ad for £1 a week. He was very sympathetic, but he explained that he was already committed to advertising in the Cumbernauld Courier rather than our paper. He did not have any more money for our paper," recalls Fred.

"We were pretty despondent because it would have been a feather in our caps to have got the cinema away from the Airdrie & Coatbridge Advertiser. We were sitting in the car outside the cinema just talking about the situation when the Kirkintilloch Herald was mentioned. Suddenly we decided to go and see if we could just buy out the paper, not for any reason except that it covered Cumbernauld too."

The two men drove to the print-works at Kirkintilloch, on the north side of Glasgow, to discover from the general manager that the business included the Milngavie and Bearsden Herald, and that the company had been inherited many years before by "two old ladies" who might just sell out. They did, for the princely sum of £20,000. The two newspapermen - management old hand and ambitious chairman's son - were on an acquisition trail which was to set the foundation of the modern-day Johnston Press group. Johnston himself had no inkling of just how big his empire might become. Incidentally, the Cumbernauld News eventually forced its rival Courier out of business.

Soon, the Ayrshire publisher Arthur Guthrie & Sons, publisher of the Ardrossan and Saltcoats Herald and some related titles, was put up for sale. George Outram's offered £45,000, while the crafty Falkirk duo bid £46,500. The strategy, very much opportunist, continued, so that by 1973, when Fred took over as chairman after his father's death, the company had bought the Fife Free Press too.

By now the Scottish weekly newspaper market, especially in the Central Belt, was dominated by Johnston and George Outram, which owned the Glasgow Herald and Evening Times, and had spun off its weekly titles into a group called Scottish & Universal Newspapers. Then part of the empire built by the late Lord Fraser of Allander, S&UN was absorbed into Lonrho during the late 1970s, and later sold to the Chester-based group Trinity International.

Local newspapers continue to thrive in Scotland. For many years they have been a first-class training ground for journalists, and while many of them would have moved on quickly to the national media, pay and conditions have improved to the extent that many others now remain working "local", carving out careers with healthily profitable papers like the Falkirk Herald, Hamilton Advertiser, and Ayrshire Post.

Unlike the English regional groups, the Scottish weekly sector has been largely unaffected by the growth of commercial local radio or the insidious spread of "free-sheets", a genre which Johnston describes as "not something I have ever been very keen on", although free papers have become a significant part of the company's English portfolio. It seems that Scots rely heavily on "parish pump" news, perhaps reflecting the close-knit nature of many urban communities in places like Lanarkshire, Stirlingshire, and Fife. During the last decade, having suffered terribly at the hands of the free-sheets and other competitive elements, the English local press has also experienced commercial revival.

Growth continued apace for Johnston during the 1970s, but the most significant purchase was the company's first venture south of the Border in 1978, when it bought the Derbyshire Times, "a big breakthrough" according to Fred. The company paid £1.5m, outbidding the mighty Yorkshire based group United Newspapers. It was to start a series of border raids which helped establish Johnston Press as a premier regional newspaper group.

One of the keys to success has been a pragmatism which Johnston is more likely to have picked up from his mentor, McGowran, rather than from his more eccentric forebears. Johnston Press has thrived by sticking to the business it knows best, local newspapers. Apart from a book-binding business, the firm remains thirled to the local press wherever its activities lie geographically. Not for Fred the grand gesture of bidding for one or other of the national newspaper groups which have changed hands during the last 15 years. This is no egotistical press baron.

Despite the couthy "local" touch to Johnston Press, there is little room for sentimentality. The Guthrie Group was sold off (and has since changed hands again) not because it was unsuccessful, but simply because its titles were not market leaders in their home area, Ayrshire, whose market was dominated by two weekly Scottish & Universal Newspapers-owned rivals, the Ayrshire Post and Kilmarnock Standard. The Oban Times, a significant newspaper in the West Highlands, was sold off "because it really needed to be run and managed by a local proprietor who could devote his time to it".

Johnston Press has had the cash, and enjoys the positive relationship with the City and the merchant banks, to branch out into larger daily newspaper groups. When Thomson Corporation decided to dispose of Aberdeen Journals and Scotsman Publications in 1995, many pundits expected the Scottish company to launch a bid. Yet Johnston steadfastly refused to consider the deal, and reputedly did not even register an interest at any stage, much to the surprise of the market, which was alive with rumour.

"Our speciality is local newspapers. They are the lifeblood of their communities. We understand them and how they work, and we prefer to act in areas where our paper is the market leader. It is a simple principle which has served us well," remarks the chairman. Significantly, he can contrast his company's actions in 1996, when it coolly borrowed £150m from its bank to buy the EMAP chain at a time when Caledonian Publishing - owner of the

Herald and Glasgow Evening Times - was struggling through the effects of the daily newspapers' price war and abandoned a Stock Market flotation to succumb to takeover by Scottish Television. In that environment, who can possibly criticise the Johnston strategy?

He may not be sentimental, but he does admit to one exception within the company's burgeoning newspaper stable. "I often say that the only things in my life with no price are my wife's virtue and the ownership of the Falkirk Herald. My wife Ann is pleased at least that I put her first in that equation." Johnston, avuncular, not afraid to digress from a business conversation to launch a wide ranging discussion on British politics, corruption in high places, and Britain's role in Europe, delivers the joke absolutely deadpan. His is a style which amuses and bewitches his shareholders and City commentators, who cannot seem to get enough of the Johnston magic.

As the 1980s' trend of mergers and acquisition grew apace, Johnston Press was in the race. By this time Tom McGowran had retired, but the burgeoning firm was run by just three men - chairman Fred, his managing director Iain Bell, and finance director Marco Chiappelli. Together they bought the Bury Times in 1983, the Yorkshire Weekly Newspaper Group in Wakefield in 1985, and the West Sussex County Times group in 1987. There were additional purchases in Derbyshire and neighbouring Nottinghamshire.

The question of flotation continued to arise. Fred has two brothers: Jim, for many years a journalist with The Scotsman, and Harry, who remains a non-executive director, and who runs the company's long standing Ford motor dealership, Craighall Garage in Edinburgh ("The company runs a fleet of 1,200 vehicles, and the dealership manages that as well as serving the retail trade," explains Fred, as if every public company with a large car fleet might as well own such a dealership).

With hindsight, although it ultimately removed family control from this essentially "family" company, flotation became inevitable. The diversity of share holdings which had resulted from the company's age and its history had become a problem, and one not uncommon in family businesses. With each generation, shares are often passed around, bequeathed, and spread across the world. A daughter marries, and the shares pass to her children, a cousin dies and leaves his shares to a more distant relative. For years, many firms have been forced to sell out or at least lose control simply because peripheral relatives want to make money from their shares. For those family members still engaged in the company's activities, this can be a real headache. So-called "succession management" and the retention of control in family businesses is now a major area of activity for accountants and consultancies specialising in advice to owner-managed companies.

Immediate family members held around 72 per cent of Johnston Press by the mid 1980s. "We needed to establish a proper market for the shares to allow some people to make money if they wished to," explains Fred. "We had witnessed many other examples where a business had to be sold to satisfy the majority. So our flotation in 1988 was aimed at achieving the best of both worlds."

After flotation, the Johnston family still had a majority of shares, but that total diminished because of rights issues and shares placements made to fund further growth, mainly by acquisition. Johnston is rightly sensitive about the portrayal of this as a family business (the family now holds less than 30 per cent) but it remains a fact that the family connection continues to be strong, and undoubtedly helps the company's public image.

This is no Stock Market player stuffed with management fat cats on high performance bonuses. Its head office has only around a dozen people, and its first action on acquiring a new business is usually in clearing out its senior management and administration in favour of the "lean machine" as Johnston describes it. It may be his journalistic background, or simply good commercial sense, but Johnston has also been reluctant to seek massive cost savings in editorial departments, reasoning that a newspaper's content is as valuable to its readers as its advertising income is to its proprietor.

Johnston's expansion has continued at explosive pace during the 1990s, at a time when British regional newspaper groups have been bought and sold or merged at staggering speed. Big companies like Thomson Corporation and Reed International have withdrawn from the market, while aggressive newcomers like Trinity and Johnston have moved in to share the spoils.

By 1996, Johnston was the 12th largest UK regional group and one of the biggest independents. It had acquired Halifax Courier Holdings for £31m in 1994, the newspaper interests of W.&J. Linney for £20m in 1995, and several South Yorkshire titles from Newsquest Media for £15m in April 1996. Pretax profits and earnings per share had grown each year since 1990, and in 1995 its newspaper division made operating profits of £13.7m on sales of £58.1m, representing an operating margin of more than 23 per cent: very high by industry standards.

In addition, the company had expanded into book binding and created a division which supplies books to public libraries. Its interests spread from Scotland to Yorkshire and beyond as far as Australia.

The big breakthrough came in April 1996. Fred and Ann Johnston were on holiday in New York City. Fred's Edinburgh based personal assistant called to say that Robin Miller, the chief executive of EMAP, one of Britain's biggest regional groups, wanted to meet and discuss selling off his company's newspapers. EMAP wanted to leave the sector, and raise money to concentrate on its magazine interests and develop its activities in electronic online services.

The EMAP chief executive said he wanted preliminary offers within a week, and told Johnston he had invited several companies to consider making bids. Johnston, the man who drove off to Kirkintilloch 33 years previously on the off-chance that a couple of old ladies might sell out their newspaper shares, operated on the same instincts, but on a grander scale. He and Ann departed for London on Concorde - "at our own expense", he adds - and he met Miller for a drink at a hotel near Heathrow Airport.

Johnston does not believe in complicating matters when it comes to bidding for a company. He just offers whatever he thinks it is worth: in the case of the EMAP newspaper group that was a breathtaking £211m, far more than any previous acquisition and more than his own company was worth. The deal was to push Johnston into the top five of the UK regional newspaper publishers' league and double its annual turnover.

Between April 17 and May 28, Johnston's team - Bell had retired from the company and been replaced by Tim Bowdler, but Chiappelli remains after more than 20 years - had prepared a package which included a £150m loan from the Royal Bank of Scotland. They were competing with several bidders including most notably the Birmingham-based Midland Independent Newspapers group.

On May 28, the two sides met at the City headquarters of Johnston's merchant bank, Hill Samuel. Before the meeting was over, Johnston and Miller shook hands on a deal, which was confirmed publicly six days later to the glee of Johnston's City supporters, and pushed the Scottish company firmly into the big league.

Predictably, Johnston's first move was to close EMAP's newspaper HQ in Stamford, Lincolnshire, a decision which will probably save the company more than £1m a year. "Fred does not like the idea of a lot of managers sitting around doing nothing, so they are always first to go," comments a long-standing admirer. And the company reorganised itself into seven divisions as well as expanding its board to include two well-respected media figures, Harry Roche of Guardian Media Group and James Gordon of Scottish Radio Holdings, the founder of Radio Clyde.

The EMAP titles included four evening newspapers in Peterborough, Northampton, Kettering, and Scarborough, plus 30 "paid for" weekly papers and 31 free newspapers. The deal would have brought a smile to the face of Tom McGowran, still living in Linlithgow and reputed to keep a friendly eye on the business he helped build when Johnston's deals were all rather simpler to complete.

Although the scale of the company is far greater, Johnston still believes in keeping things simple. Apart from book-binding, his company's newspaper interests are managed on a divisional basis, including Scotland, the English Midlands, North and South of England, Midlands/East Anglia, Isle of Man, Yorkshire, and Sussex. Each division has a director with a small management team, reporting to Tim Bowdler in Edinburgh headquarters, a discreet Georgian town-house in the city's Manor Place.

In conversation, Fred Johnston will give voice to his concerns about social breakdown, about the menace of anti-European sentiment in British politics, and his deteriorating opinion of the Conservative Party. He will wax lyrically about old railways, having become something of an expert on the history of the Irish system: "Did you know that the Irish railways run on a different gauge because the various companies had all developed their own different types of track and the colonial governor compromised by ordering a standard gauge which was completely different from all of them, and from the British mainland?" he asks. "So all trains in Ireland run on a different gauge from anywhere else. It really is fascinating." What he means, probably, is that such an apparent folly appeals to the Johnston humour.

He retains a journalist's eye on current events, although his mind is that of an amiable but ruthless deal-maker. He believes in full disclosure of company accounts, and will happily tell any visitor details of his salary or share options, adding: "I believe in corporate agreement, and I do not believe in conspicuous consumption." He is in some respects a most unlikely media mogul, but an incredibly successful one at that.

His work in Edinburgh is carried out under the watchful eye of great-uncle Fred, the man who righted the company's wrongs a century ago, immortalised in oils and hung on the wall near chairman Fred's desk. The old man is depicted with a copy of the Falkirk Herald in his lap: he took over the company in 1882 after buying out the shares of his brothers, who were all strapped for cash. That was clearly an entrepreneur's instinct which his great-nephew inherited and has put to such good use over the last 30 years.

The Johnston name is likely to survive within the company in years to come. Fred has two sons, one of whom Robert worked in magazines in Australia before returning to London, where he edits the Sunday Times' Style section. Michael, aged 34, spent 13 years with the BBC, latterly as a current affairs producer, and has now joined Johnston Press as a management trainee in the company's Chesterfield division. "This is no silver spoon situation," says his father. "He will make his own way in the company, or not at all."

Time will tell whether Michael proves to be a chip off the old block and rise high enough to ensure that, even as a public company, Johnston Press continues its third century with a Johnston descendant helping to run one of Scotland's unsung success stories.